Rallying the Really Human Things

The Moral Imagination in Politics, Literature, and Everyday Life

Vigen Guroian

ISI Books · Wilmington, Delaware

Library of Congress Cataloging-in-Publication Data:

Guroian, Vigen.

    Rallying the really human things : the moral imagination in politics, literature, and everyday life / Vigen Guroian. — 1st ed. — Wilmington, Del. : ISI Books, c2005.

        p. ; cm.
        Includes bibliographical references and index.
        ISBN: 193223649X
        1932236503 (pbk.)

        1. Christian ethics. 2. Humanism. 3. Imagination (Philosophy) 4. Philosophy, Modern. 5. Humanistic ethics. 6. Humanism in literature. 7. Political ethics. 8. Transcendentalism. I. Title.

BJ1251 .G87 2005   2004104756
241—dc22   0506

ISI Books
Intercollegiate Studies Institute
P.O. Box 4431
Wilmington, DE 19807-0431
www.isibooks.org

Book design by Kara Beer

Manufactured in the United States of America

Dedicated in gratitude
to Russell and Annette Kirk

Contents

3: Wanderings in the Wasteland

4: Politics and Freedom

Preface

"Rallying the Really Human Things" is a phrase of G. K. Chesterton's. And not by accident, I called the column in which previous versions of about half the chapters gathered here first appeared "Really Human Things." From the beginning I thought that I might compose enough essays to make up a book with Chesterton's phrase for the title. Invitations to speak at the Russell Kirk Center for Cultural Renewal reinforced this idea and gave me the opportunity to think and write more on the notion that there are certain things that are properly, "really" human.

This book, the culmination of that activity, admittedly has neither the unity nor the coherence of a conventional monograph. Rather, it includes essays on a variety of topics. There is a guiding vision, however, one best conveyed by the interrelated themes of Christian humanism and the moral imagination, themes explored in depth in the first five chapters. My choice of the trio of G. K. Chesterton (1874–1936), Flannery O'Connor (1925–64), and Russell Kirk (1918–94) as representative Christian humanists is somewhat arbitrary, but it is not without justification. For many years, I have turned to G. K. Chesterton not only for Christian instruction, but also because he is a master of English prose style. Flannery O'Connor's reputation as an American fiction writer grows in stature with each passing decade. She remains a mainstay of my college courses in theology and literature, for she shines as a brilliant star of the Christian imagination. I first became acquainted with Russell Kirk through his writings. In high school I read his best-known work, *The Conservative Mind* (1953), and carried it with me to college. Later on, I got to know Dr. Kirk personally and also edited and introduced a collection of his richly imaginative gothic ghost stories, recently published as *Ancestral Shadows: An Anthology of Ghostly Tales* (2004).

Each of these three modern figures, in his or her own unique way, casts the light of the profound tradition of Christian humanism onto the dark wood of our time. Chesterton, O'Connor, and Kirk offer a vision of the human good that unmasks the metaphysical and moral bankruptcy of a secular humanism riddled with relativism and lurching toward nihilism.

The fourth and fifth chapters in this volume define, discuss, and critically employ the term "moral imagination." Edmund Burke (1729–97) is credited with first introducing this phrase in his *Reflections on the Revolution in France.* The Harvard scholar Irving Babbitt (1865–1933) used it effectively in his literary and social criticism, and Russell Kirk, consciously following them both, embraced it in his cultural and literary analysis. Kirk contrasted the moral imagination with the corrupted forms of imagination that thrive in late modernity: the idyllic imagination, which Irving Babbitt discusses in *Rousseau and Romanticism,* and the diabolic imagination, which T. S. Eliot (1888–1965) describes in *After Strange Gods.* In chapter 4, I add another corrupted form of imagination to this list: the idolatrous imagination.

Chesterton's "really human things" may be defined as certain perennial powers and attributes of human existence, perennial because they express the given nature of that creature whom God has created in his own image. Modern man misuses and mars these distinctively human things through his hubris and impiety. Sophocles and Shakespeare both teach us that this sort of pride and impiety is the path to tragedy. The abuse of our sexual nature and procreative powers, the undermining of the biblical and Christian understanding of marriage and the family, the rape of nature, the moral and intellectual evisceration of liberal education, the degradation of work and misspent leisure—all are signs of our cultural decadence.

Secularism, which penetrates and permeates contemporary culture, breeds moral relativism and coarsens our common life. Liberal utilitarianism and pragmatism employ a shallow rhetoric of personal rights and liberties and freedom of choice. This book is intended, in part, to show that something more than appeal to human reason or sentiment is needed to secure fundamental human liberties in a social order that honors and protects the dignity of the human person. The religious and moral imaginations must be brought into play.

The chapters under the third heading, "Wanderings in the Wasteland," address various sectors of everyday life. The heading, of course, is an allusion to T. S. Eliot's great literary monument, "The Wasteland." In these essays, I assume the role of that poem's sojourner-searcher, who climbs over, picks up, and reflects upon the broken shards of our culture and civilization, and who also observes the death of lasting love and communion in modern life. This search becomes an act of recovery, the recovery and articulation of an organizing and integrating vision of life.

Finally, I close this volume with several essays on politics. The four essays collected in the "Politics and Freedom" section are chiefly concerned with meaning in politics and the norms that enable human community to flourish. The first of these essays investigates the nature of political rhetoric and how such rhetoric might successfully articulate a moving vision of purposeful political existence. In other chapters, I consider from whence come the norms that support just and healthy human community. I conclude that the modern doctrines of human rights and human autonomy are not adequate to the goal of securing human freedom and respect for the dignity of the human person. Thus, I return to the theme of the first chapters, that a transcendent, even religious dimension to human life must be believed, articulated, and acted upon in the political order if a humane society is to persist and prosper.

Acknowledgments

I hold the strongest opinion that a fresh and confident editorial hand is a gift of great value to an author. I have been fortunate in this regard. Thus, I want to thank several persons who played a special role in the formation of this book and its publication. As I mention in the preface, a substantial number of early versions of chapters first appeared under a column I wrote from 2001 to 2003 for the Prison Fellowship Ministries' *Wilberforce* and *Breakpoint* websites. These include chapters 1, 2, 4, 7, 10, and 14. During this time, two extremely talented young editors, Douglas C. Minson and Peter L. Edman, did a wonderful job of cleaning up and enhancing what I had written. They also encouraged me and lent their considerable editorial skills to what you have before you. Likewise, chapter 13, "Why Should Businessmen Read Great Literature?" was first published in *Religion and Liberty* in summer 2002. Gregory Dunn, another very talented young editor, not only put his hand to the text but initially presented me with the idea for the essay.

Versions of chapters 1, 2, and 5 appeared in the *Intercollegiate Review*.

The first two were expanded from essays I had written for the previously mentioned column. Chapters 8 and 11 were first published in *Touchstone* magazine. Chapter 15 is drawn from the book *Sovereignty at the Crossroads: Morality and International Politics in the Post–Cold War Era* (Lanham, MD: Rowman and Littlefield, 1996), edited by Luis E. Lugo. Chapter 16 appeared in the fall 1998 issue of the *Journal of Religious Ethics* and chapter 17 in the *Annual of the Society of Christian Ethics* (1997).

In conclusion, I want to express special thanks to Annette Kirk and through her to her late husband Russell Kirk. Our relationship goes back thirty years. With respect to this book, however, Annette in particular encouraged me to think and write about its central themes by inviting me to speak on them at seminars held at the Russell Kirk Center for Cultural Renewal in Mecosta, Michigan. Also, I owe much gratitude to Jeffrey O. Nelson, publisher of ISI Books, for his friendship and for his wish that I put together this volume.

· *1* ·

Three Voices
of
Christian Humanism

1

G. K. Chesterton:

Rallying the Really Human Things

W e need a rally of the really *human* things; will which is morals, memory which is tradition, culture which is the mental thrift of the fathers."[1] That was the judgment of G. K. Chesterton some seventy years ago in an essay titled "Is Humanism a Religion?" In order to rally the really human things, Chesterton proposed a new Christian humanism, while he simultaneously warned of the dangers and deceptions of a popular secular humanism that behaved as if it were a religion.

Chesterton distinguished this modern secular humanism from a much older tradition of Christian humanism, with which he strongly identified. The headwaters of this Christian humanism are the writings of such ancient church fathers as Basil of Caesarea and John Chrysostom, Saint Augustine and Gregory the Great. The stream is replenished by such late-medieval and early-Renaissance figures as Dante, Erasmus, and Thomas More. Chesterton extols the efforts of these humanists. "I doubt," he writes, "if any thinking person, of any belief or unbelief, does not wish in his heart that the end of mediaevalism had meant the triumph of the Humanists like Erasmus and More."[2]

In recent decades "secular humanism" has become a term of opprobrium among conservative Christians who identify it with the forces they believe are undermining the religious foundations of Western civilization. Chesterton's criticism is aimed more specifically at the philosophical outlooks of significant writers of his own time, including Aldous Huxley, George Bernard Shaw, and H. G. Wells. He admires all of these men for their often insightful social criticism and their literary talent. But he ultimately rejects their brand of humanism because it is entirely anthropocentric.

True humanism, argues Chesterton, is theocentric. Christian humanism honors the fact that, though created of dust, the human being is the only creature made by God in his very own image and likeness. Christian humanism answers humankind's need to be redeemed from a fallen condition in which this image is tarnished, and in which death works like a rust that destroys even the most beautiful bronze statue. Because it knows the difference between God and man and the effects of sin, Christian humanism rejects the spurious notions of human progress and perfection espoused by secular humanists. Christian humanism builds upon the human person's "inner-directedness" toward the transcendent. It nurtures and disciplines this yearning (*eros*) for the divine life—for truth, goodness, and beauty—that God has planted in every human being.

Christian humanism is grounded in the doctrine of the Incarnation and gains its special character from that doctrine. God in Christ affirms our enfleshed and historical existence and gives meaning to it in spite of death. Within human culture and through the elements of this material world—bread and wine, oil and water, flesh and blood—the incarnate Son saves us body and soul from sin and death. God has given human beings compelling reasons to labor with him and within and through this physical world to redeem the whole of creation.

These Christian facts, Chesterton agues, are the inspiration of Christian humanism, which stands in contrast to man-centered philosophies of life that embrace matter to the exclusion of spirit, or else reject the material world in a flight to something deemed "spiritual." Such secularist philosophies are not necessarily atheistic, but they cannot sustain either faith in a personal God or belief in the dignity, freedom, and eternal worth of the human person. The loss of this faith is the principal symptom, argues Chesterton, of the decline of the Christian paradoxical imagination.

The loss of the paradoxical vision and the crisis of secular humanism

In the introduction to his edited volume *The New Religious Humanists*, Gregory Wolfe argues that in the history of Western culture "religious humanism has made only infrequent appearances and has rarely occupied center stage." He explains that it "is a mode of thought that tends to arise when cultural cohesion is threatened by large social and intellectual upheavals."[3] He regards the time in which we live as one such moment. Wolfe adds that Christian humanism mediates the human and divine and the temporal and the eternal through paradox and thus avoids the Gnostic proclivities of secular ideology.

> On the face of it, the term religious humanism seems to suggest a tension between two opposed terms—heaven and earth, so to speak. But this is a creative, rather than a deconstructive, tension. Perhaps the best analogy for understanding religious humanism comes from the Christian doctrine of the Incarnation, which holds that Jesus was both human and divine. In the paradoxical meeting of Christ's two natures is the pattern by which we can begin to understand the many dualities we experience in life: flesh and spirit, nature and grace, God and Caesar, faith and reason, justice and mercy.[4]

Chesterton is perhaps the most articulate twentieth-century practitioner of this Christian paradoxical imagination. He judges that a serious breakdown of the fundamental moral suppositions deposited by biblical faith and the classical tradition is underway and accelerating. He believes that this declension is due to a loss of conviction in our culture about the reality of the Incarnation—that God truly became a human being in Jesus Christ—with all the import that that event has for human existence. For Chesterton, the doctrine of the Incarnation is the hinge that holds together what is, for the Christian, a vision of the world that is essentially paradoxical. And he is astonishingly adept at employing this vision in his cultural criticism and Christian apologetics. The Incarnation sheds light where sin deceives and despair darkens the human horizon. Sin causes us to experience spirit in opposition to matter, faith in conflict with reason, life defeated by death. But the Incarnation reveals these apparent contradictions as paradoxes.

Contradiction may signal futility, but paradox is pregnant with the possibility of resolution and harmony. Paradox is an ally of truth. The good news of the Christian Gospel is that the God who is spirit became flesh, that infinite being became finite existence, that the immortal One became mortal man in order that death might be undone and humanity drawn into eternal life. God in his being and act unties the Gordian knot of sin. The errors of pagan religion and the falsehoods of atheistic and antihuman secularism are exposed by the Incarnation and replaced by its paradoxical truth. This divine and human truth opens a way for man, an alternative to the escape of the soul from matter and time or the embrace of mere flesh and finitude in a courtship with personal extinction.

Chesterton believes that the collapse of this wonderful vision of man in his relation to both heaven and earth lies at the heart of the modern crisis of meaning. Indeed, what makes Chesterton instructive today is that he lived on the cusp of postmodernity. Modernity was the result of a five-hundred-year process in which the dual Christian truth about the dignity and degradation of human existence, illuminated by the Incarnation, held together by the paradoxical imagination, was split apart. Secularist humanism emerged from this fractured truth and has not known how to put it back together, even when it has desired to do so. It seems doomed, rather, to fly from one pole of that truth to the other. On the one hand, it seeks to affirm, through some form of idealism or other, the "divinity" of human life, yet it rejects the doctrine of the Incarnation. On the other hand, it is drawn toward the opposite pole of naturalism and relativism and forgets the crucial difference between finitude and sin—and the distinctions between error and contravention of higher law. Chesterton sums up:

> Where is the cement which made religion corporate and popular, which can prevent [humanism] falling to pieces in a debris of individualistic tastes and degrees? What is to prevent one Humanist wanting chastity, and another truth, or beauty without either? The problem of an enduring ethic and culture consists in finding an arrangement of the pieces by which they remain related, as do the stones in an arch. I know of only one scheme that has thus proved its solidity, bestriding lands and ages with its gigantic arches, and carrying everywhere the high river of baptism upon an aqueduct to Rome.[5]

In its late-Renaissance and Enlightenment origins, secular humanism is still a "mitigated" Christian humanism in which God is driven to the borders of human life and enterprise. Grace is redefined as "the supernatural varnish of those acts whose perfect rectitude the *reason* of the upright man suffices to assure," notes Jacques Maritain.[6] Eventually, nature becomes the sole norm, as perfection entails not a transcendent participation in the life of God but is rather completely imminent. The modern idea of progress emerges, justified by an unquestioning faith in reason and modern science. In the nineteenth and twentieth centuries, this secular humanism embraces a complete human autonomy that needs neither God nor grace.

Chesterton's life straddled the nineteenth and twentieth centuries. This provided him a vantage point from which to see the line that was being crossed in his time. The old idealistic liberal humanism born of the Renaissance and Enlightenment was giving way to a militant, anti-theistic secularism, whose child is nihilism. He judges that all of the principal spheres of culture, the family, education, economic life, and politics are being hollowed out and vacated of moral conviction by the solvent of rationalism and the blindness of positivism. I do not think that he would have been surprised by the radical historicism, skepticism, and relativism espoused by contemporary postmodernists like Jacques Derrida and Richard Rorty and embraced naïvely by many ordinary people today.

In *Orthodoxy*, Chesterton quips: "At any street corner we meet a man who utters the frantic and blasphemous statement that he may be wrong. Everyday one comes across somebody who says that of course his view may not be the right one, or it is not his view. We are on the road to producing a race of men too mentally modest to believe in the multiplication table, leave aside making a sure distinction between right and wrong."[7] He concludes that secular humanism is the gathering "place" of forces that undermine the really *human* things and open the gates for anti-human ideologies dressed in shepherd's clothes. This new humanism is especially subversive and damaging to Christian faith and Western culture because it is parasitic. It exploits and expends the religious and moral capital of biblical faith and is incapable of replenishing that capital. Chesterton observes that secular humanism "is using, and using up, the truths that remain out of the old treasury of Christendom."[8] The deposit of moral truths set adrift by a disintegrating Christendom is thus gradually degraded, reduced to ideological half-truths and sappy clichés.

> The modern world is not [wholly] evil. [Indeed], in some ways the modern world is far too good. It is full of wild and wasted virtues. When a religious scheme is shattered ... it is not merely vices that are set loose. . . . But the virtues are let loose also;

and the virtues wander more wildly [than the vices], and the virtues do more terrible damage. The modern world is full of the old Christian virtues gone mad. The virtues have gone mad because they have been isolated from each other and are wandering alone.[9]

Consider the Christian virtue of charity, for example. Instead of the selfless seeking of another's good, charity becomes sugary sentiment. It is invoked to deny that forgiveness entails judgment and repentance, or that sin even exists. In due course, secular humanism may rob or empty all of the virtues of their true and vital meaning. The final outcome of such a process can be seen in what has been done to the religious notion of the dignity of human life. It has been uprooted from its biblical ground and the garden of the church. Its deep *human* meaning, nurtured by the Christian doctrine of the *imago Dei*, withers and fades from memory. A desiccated concept of human dignity is embraced instead. And ironically, or rather tragically, that concept is deployed to justify acts that contradict traditional moral teaching.

Chesterton says that the humanism of the secularist leads morality down a perilous path, a path that he tells us in *Orthodoxy* is paved with pragmatism and relativism. Man is told "to think what he must and never mind the Absolute." "But precisely one of the things he must think," adds Chesterton, "is the Absolute." Otherwise, the whole of the rest of the world is an illusion. Both pragmatism and relativism embrace an outlook "just as inhuman as the determinism" to which they often vehemently object. "The determinist (who, to do him justice, does not pretend to be a human being) makes nonsense of the human sense of actual choice." But pragmatism and relativism "make nonsense of the human sense of fact."[10] The road they pave leads to the devil's version of the Emerald City, where nothing is what it seems, words are no longer tools of truth but instruments of raw power, and the moral compass is abandoned because there are no true poles of good and evil or right and wrong.

This suicide of thought, as Chesterton calls it, leads inexorably toward the denial of the existence of the good—or of anything that is really and permanently human. In 1905, in a book titled *Heretics*, Chesterton anticipates with uncanny prescience what postmodernism at the turn of the twenty-first century boldly declares. "Modern morality," he writes, seems only capable of making a case for itself by pointing out "the horrors that follow breaches of law."[11] Premarital sex may be inadvisable because one risks pregnancy or AIDS. One probably shouldn't lie because lying undercuts the social trust that is the precondition for getting what one really wants. All of these "prohibitions" are subject, of course, to alteration or negation if means may be found to avoid negative consequences. In other words, modern morality is consequentialist. More than that, it is morbidly consequentialist, having lost a sure vision of the goodness of goodness.

In the end, images of automobile accidents, pictures of people dying from AIDS, and photographs of aborted fetuses won't necessarily stop people from drinking and driving, engaging in casual or "unprotected" sex, or escaping the inconvenience of having a child by having an abortion. At the Creation, God did not say: *I will make the seas with clean water, not polluted water, and the land arable and not desert because it would be a disaster for the environment otherwise.* He made the seas clean and the land habitable because it was good that they be so. A vision of the good has far greater power to move men and women to do the right thing than all the horrible images we may conjure up to terrify them into doing it.

In *Heretics*, Chesterton observes: "A young man may keep himself from vice by continually thinking of disease. He may keep himself from it also by continually thinking of the Virgin Mary. There may be question about which method is the more reasonable, or even about which is the more efficient. But surely there can be no question about which is the more wholesome."[12] Modern people, he says, have grown so modest about the good that they no longer believe they can be certain of what it is. Erroneous notions of tolerance are fostered by secular humanism in its final stage as it gives itself over to nihilism. Even ordinary people voice the opinion that our principal moral obligation is not to believe too strongly in any moral conviction. "A great silent collapse, an enormous unspoken disappointment has, in our time, fallen on our . . . civilization," writes Chesterton. "All previous ages have sweated and been crucified in an attempt to realize what is really the good man. [Yet] a definite part of the modern world has come . . . to the conclusion that there is no answer to these questions."[13] Under the aegis of secular humanism, an idea which is inherently absurd gains support: that human flourishing may be achieved without defining what is human or what is good for human beings. Chesterton continues:

> Every one of the popular modern phrases and ideals is a dodge in order to shirk the problem of what is good. We are fond of talking about "liberty"; that, as we talk of it, is a dodge to avoid discussing what is good. We are fond of talking about "progress"; that is a dodge to avoid discussing what is good. We are fond about talking about "education"; that is a dodge to avoid discussing what is good. The modern man says, "Let us leave all these arbitrary standards and embrace liberty." This is, logically rendered, "Let us not decide what is good, but let it be considered good not to decide it." He says, "Away with your old moral formulae; I am for progress." This, logically stated, means, "Let us not settle what is good; but let us settle whether we are getting more of it." He says, "Neither in religion nor in morality, my friend, lie the hopes of the race, but in education." This, clearly expressed, means, "We cannot decide what is good, but let us give it to our children."[14]

Many would agree that Chesterton has got hold of something disturbing about the modern temper. His diagnosis, prescient in his own time, is confirmed in ours. What drew the venom of his adversaries and continues to offend many is his prescription. Secularism needs to be replaced by faith, he says unabashedly, and relativism by firm standards of right and wrong. In the simplest terms, Chesterton proposes a return to dogma, a proposal that sounds exceedingly strange to moderns, who think that tolerance and an indiscriminant commitment to "diversity" are the highest goods of civilized life.

Joseph Wood Krutch on the modern temper

I want to explore what a return to dogma means and what its importance is for Chesterton's Christian humanism. But before doing so, it may be useful and instructive to examine in counterpoint the views of one of Chesterton's younger contemporaries. In perhaps his best-known book, titled *The Modern Temper* and published in 1929, the American literary and social critic Joseph Wood Krutch ruthlessly flayed the illusions of the liberal humanism of his day, illusions to which he himself had earlier adhered. In that book, Krutch concluded that the collapse of Western civilization is inevitable, even if the course is long and winding. Krutch's analyses of the modern crisis shared much in common with Chesterton's. But whereas Chesterton saw through the crisis to hope, Krutch crouched in despair.

Krutch's despair is especially poignant because he understands its source. His liberal and secular creed does not permit belief in the truths and verities of traditional religion. Liberated reason must do without dogma. Krutch also recognizes the terrible irony in this situation. For without faith and certitude, there is no stopping the new barbarians who are knocking down the fortress walls of the civilization he loves. With melancholic honesty Krutch writes in his book's foreword:

> I have neither celebrated the good old days nor attempted to prove that mankind is about to enter a golden age. I am sure

that those who hold conventional religious opinions will find my book in many ways offensive and I fancy that many who are militantly rationalistic will be disgusted by my failure to share their optimism concerning the future of a rationalistic humanity.... Certainly if any modern temper like that herein described does actually exist it is very different from that scientific optimism, which, though it is being widely popularized at the present moment, really belongs to nineteenth century thought and certainly one of its most distinguished features is just its inability to achieve either religious belief on the one hand or exultant atheism on the other. Unlike their grandfathers, those who are its victims do not and never expect to believe in God; but unlike their spiritual fathers, the philosophers and scientists of the nineteenth century, they have begun to doubt that rationality and knowledge have any promised land into which they may be led.[15]

There is something at once noble and pathetic about this declaration. For Krutch concedes that he himself has contributed to the subversion of the foundations of liberal society. This is because he and other secular liberals are unable to believe in or to commend to others the truths and moral principles that inspire a free society and give men and women reasons to defend it. "The world may be rejuvenated in one way or another, but we will not," Krutch confesses. "Skepticism has entered too deeply into our souls ever to be replaced by faith, and we can never forget the things which the new barbarians will never need to know."[16]

Scientific enlightenment, says Krutch, makes it no longer possible to hold to the classical and biblical belief that the virtues participate in a larger transcendent purpose. Human ignorance and fear imagined a meaningful universe masked in mystery and headed toward salvation; we must now conclude that the universe is impersonal and indifferent to human purpose or suffering. "It is no longer [possible] to believe or tell tales of noble men because we do not believe that noble men exist [nor the gods they would obey]. The best we can do is achieve pathos and the most that we can do is to feel sorry for ourselves.... [The] cosmos may be farcical or it may be pathetic but it has not [even] the dignity of tragedy."[17] The human cause, says Krutch, "is a lost cause ... [as] there is no place for us in the natural universe." But for the stoic Krutch, "we are not, for all that, sorry to be human. We should rather die as men than live as animals."[18]

In the final analysis, Krutch's humanism collapses upon itself. The humanist who values human freedom so highly ironically subverts freedom's transcendent foundations with a deadly embrace of naturalism or radical historicism. Under either, freedom is an illusion, much as God is a projection of the human mind. We are left to believe and behave as if there is more than there really is—that our humanity is special and our freedom is real—because to believe and act in any other manner would be unpleasant. "We have discovered the trick which has been played upon us," Krutch declares, "and ... are [at least] no longer dupes."[19]

A return to dogma

So far as I am aware, Chesterton did not review *The Modern Temper*. But let me speculate as to how he might have answered Krutch. I suspect that Chesterton would have begun by observing that Krutch rejects religious revelation and truth too hastily. Even as he claims that theism has been irreversibly demythologized, Krutch himself is caught in the myth of secularist liberalism. He is like a man blindfolded who thinks that the object of his criticism has disappeared, or like the child who thinks that he has hidden from his playmates by covering his eyes with his hands. In *The Modern Temper*, Krutch criticizes both Chesterton and T. S. Eliot for taking "refuge" in Roman and Anglican Catholicism, "whose dogmas, if accepted without argument, provide the basis which pure reason cannot discover."[20]

However, if one reads Chesterton carefully and fairly (and Eliot as well) one sees that his diagnosis of modernity is neither romantic nor reactionary. Chesterton knows that Christendom is gone and that the church no longer stands at the center of culture. Indeed, he chides those who continue to think triumphantly that England is still a Christian nation.[21] Nowhere does he suggest that his aim is to put the old Christendom back together again, in England or anywhere else.

Krutch's honesty and despair, in fact, support Chesterton's contention that secular humanism at the ship's helm has at great peril thrown overboard the spiritual ballast of civilized life and broken religion's moral compass. As the ship rocks and tips to the deep, the humanist's talk of there being "no precise moral ideals . . . [sounds] ludicrous." For progress cannot be charted without sure points of reference and a compass. Chesterton writes:

> I do not . . . say that the word "progress" is unmeaning; I say that it is unmeaning without the previous definition of a moral doctrine, and that it can only be applied to groups of persons who hold that doctrine in common. Progress is not an illegitimate word, but it is logically evident that it is illegitimate for us. It is a sacred word, a word that could only rightly be used by rigid believers and in the ages of faith.[22]

Here, surely, is the nub of the matter. Chesterton's turn to dogma is not what it sounds like to the ears of secularists, modern and postmodern. He does not say that we must believe in dogmas or else the worst. He does not force dogma down our throats. He does not offer dogma as a bulwark against regress or decline. Rather, dogma—religious truth affirmed in consensus, established in authority, and declared as norm in public debate—is bound to reemerge precisely because human beings cannot live and prosper in a world in which truth is thought not to exist. In *Heretics* Chesterton explains:

Man can be defined as an animal that makes dogmas. As he piles doctrine on doctrine and conclusion on conclusion in the formation of some tremendous scheme of philosophy and religion, he is, in the only legitimate sense ... becoming more and more human. When he drops one doctrine after another in a refined scepticism, when he says that he has outgrown definitions, when he says that he disbelieves in finality, when, in his own imagination, he sits as God, holding to no form of creed and contemplating all, then he is by that very process sinking slowly backwards into the vagueness of the vagrant animals and the unconsciousness of grass. Trees have no dogmas. Turnips are singularly broad-minded.[23]

A postmodern world requires a Christian humanism grounded in philosophical realism. Chesterton judges that people are ready for it, for a fraud has been perpetrated. The skeptics contradict themselves. They oppose dogma dogmatically and deny their own humanity in doing it. They claim to be empirical but deny the testimony of lives lived in faith. The seeds of suspicion they sow can also sprout, however, into fresh seedlings of belief.

When will we know that the rally for the really *human* things has begun in earnest? With the return of dogma, of course. And Chesterton is as sure of a return to dogma as he is that birds need air in which to fly and that fish need water in which to swim. At the close of *Heretics*, he sounds what Robert Royal has called "the battle charge for the kind of struggle"[24] that must necessarily ensue if humanity is to avoid the abyss of postmodern nihilism and return to a God-centered vision of human nature and destiny. This is what Chesterton says:

Truths turn into dogmas the instant that they are disputed. Thus every man who utters a doubt defines a religion. And the scepticism of our time does not really destroy the beliefs, rather it creates them; gives them limits and their plain and

defiant shape. . . . We who are Christians never knew the great
philosophic common sense which inheres in that mystery until
the anti-Christian writers pointed it out to us. The great march
of mental destruction will go on. Everything will be denied.
Everything will become a creed. It is a reasonable position to
deny the stones in the street; it will be a religious dogma to
assert them. It is a rational thesis that we are all in a dream; it
will be a mystical sanity to say that we are all awake. Fires
will be kindled to testify that two and two make four. Swords
will be drawn to prove that leaves are green in summer. We
will be defending not only the incredible virtues and sanities
of human life, but something more incredible still, this huge
impossible universe which stares us in the face. We shall fight
for the visible prodigies of the invisible. We shall look on the
impossible grass and the skies with a strange courage. We shall
be those who have seen and yet have believed.[25]

Chesterton challenges us with one final paradox. Without dogma, there
is merely descent into chaos and nothingness. With dogma, we may become demons in bellicose combat over many truths and many gods. For in
a sinful world dogma comes into combat with dogma. Nevertheless, dogma,
the right dogma, may also enable us to be godlike, to recognize ourselves
as creatures made in the image of the one God who must live in the unity
of his truth revealed in the flesh of a man who lived twenty centuries ago.

Contrary to so much of what claims to be Christian in our culture, we
are called to believe not in order to gain peace but to know the truth.
Dogma is religious truth, but it hardly guarantees peace. The first and last
lesson of Christian humanism is this: by our own efforts alone, we cannot
sew together the cloth of peace from our sinful and tattered human nature. Real peace, like real humanity, is a transcendent gift, which we will
enjoy only when we wholly accept and faithfully obey the God who has
become really human.

2

Flannery O'Connor:

The Art of Incarnation

Christian humanism has always served a two-pronged function, both presenting the truths of Christian doctrine and exposing the errors of the age. In the time of the early church, Christian humanism championed the doctrines of Creation, Incarnation, redemption, and the sanctification of life. At the same time, it vigorously countered the dominant currents in Hellenic culture that regarded spirit and matter as opposites in the same manner as goodness is to evil or lightness to darkness. The religion and philosophy of antiquity commonly thought of the divine as spirit, that is wholly unrelated to the material world. In other words, a wholly good—and hence wholly spiritual—God would never enter the realm of matter as Christians claimed. St. Paul alludes to this opposition in his First Epistle to the Corinthians when he describes the Christian belief in "Christ crucified" as "foolishness to Gentiles" (I Corinthians 1: 23).

Early Christian humanists such as St. Irenaeus (c.130–c.200) and St. Athanasius (c.296–373) elaborated on St. Paul's observation in their arguments with pagan critics who insisted that salvation is the liberation of the captive soul or spirit from the prison of the body. These Christian writers forcefully invoked the dogmas of the Incarnation and bodily Resurrection and Ascension of Jesus Christ to affirm the goodness of the physical creation. Their belief that the divine Word had truly become a man defined their Christianity. Their high view of the human person as enfleshed spirit destined for eternal life expressed their humanism.

This early Christian humanism was in controversy with two Christian gnostic movements, Docetism and Manicheanism, which embraced an extreme dualism of matter and spirit. Gnosticism in its various expressions and systems of thought laid claim to a special knowledge (gnosis) of God and salvation that viewed the material creation as evil. The Docetists believed that the humanity of Christ was a phantasm in which divinity "dressed" itself, and through which it communicated the knowledge of spiritual salvation to an elect. The Manicheans believed that the human body is a prison for particles of light stolen from the power of Light by Satan. These particular lights are released upon the death of the body to return to the divine Light.

In the previous chapter, I introduced G. K. Chesterton as a modern representative of Christian humanism. In this chapter I want to take up another more contemporary voice of Christian humanism who defended Christian orthodoxy against what she took to be the gnostic predilections of our own day. Flannery O'Connor was born in 1925, a decade before Chesterton's death, and she died much too young at the age of thirty-nine in 1964. Yet in her short lifetime, she produced a body of fiction that stands up as some of the best American writing of the twentieth century, writing that is imbued with a capacious Christian imagination. Whereas Chesterton's life straddled the nineteenth and twentieth century, O'Connor was wholly an inhabitant of the twentieth century. And it is as a full-time denizen of that century that she carries and advances the legacy of Christian humanism and exposes the gnostic heresy in modernity.

In her fiction, O'Connor delivered her critique of gnosticism with devastating power and wit, and I will turn to two of her short stories, "The Enduring Chill" and "Parker's Back," to demonstrate how she accomplished this. But first let me review briefly some of what Flannery O'Connor had to say about such matters elsewhere.

In an essay titled "The Nature and Aim of Fiction," O'Connor throws down the gauntlet. She states that the gnostic vision not only cuts off a serious regard for history and the created order, but cannot, if consistently adhered to, sustain the literary and moral imagination.

> The Manicheans separated spirit and matter. To them all material things were evil. They sought pure spirit and tried to approach the infinite directly without any mediation of matter. This is also pretty much the modern spirit, and for the sensibility infected with it, fiction is hard if not impossible to write because fiction is so very much an incarnational art. . . . The fact is that the materials of the fiction writer are the humblest. Fiction is about every thing human and we are made of dust.[1]

O'Connor does not dispute that our culture generates a massive appetite for the consumption of material goods and feeds an obsession with the body and sex. In this respect the age is clearly materialistic—we rightly hesitate to suggest that it views matter as evil. Nevertheless, careful consideration of this modern vision reveals several ironies that expose a spirit and body (or body and self) dualism that is akin to classical gnosticism. Consider the omnipresent modern concern for sex. While it is not reduced to mere animal intercourse, it is certainly devalued. Human sexuality is thoroughly permeated by spirit and always transcends mere instinct. But modern sex is trivialized by sentimentality or distorted into obscenity and pornography.

In "The Church and the Fiction Writer," O'Connor explains that sentimentalized sex leaps over sin to "a mock state of innocence." Obscenity is "essentially sentimental, for it leaves out the connection of sex with its hard purpose [procreation] and so far disconnects it from the meaning in life as to make it simply an experience for its own sake."[2] Sentimentalized and romanticized sex presses toward angelism, a viewpoint toward the body that implicitly, if not explicitly, denies that the body is constitutive of the self. Instead, it thinks of the body as merely an instrument of a transcendent self. In this manner the human body is radically devalued. Likewise, consumerism and the pursuit of material possessions do not satisfy people's need for a meaningful life. The mandarins of marketing and advertising know this. So they constantly fuel this dissatisfaction and inflame the acquisitive spirit with incessant promises that the next purchase will quench the craving.

The worth of creation

But modern people also seek relief and escape from chasing after material things and the syndrome of insatiable desire. And when they do, they are drawn to a plethora of mysticisms, transcendental religions, and New Age spiritualities. These "religious substitutes for religion," says O'Connor in one of her letters, lack the belief "that God has the power to do things" in this material realm. "There is no sense that the power of God could produce the Incarnation or Resurrection."[3] "Today's reader, if he believes in grace at all, sees it as something which can be separated from nature and served to him raw as instant Uplift," she writes in "Novelist and Believer."[4] Thus even if we don't find full-fledged Manichean religion in the modern world, radical dualisms of spirit and matter and nature and grace abound. The flight to spirituality is a flight from this world, while grace is considered some sort of magic wholly alien to nature.

In her fiction, O'Connor lays waste to this kind of escapism and pseudotranscendence. She endeavors to show through narrative that the only real path to human happiness is one that includes our bodies: not our bodies as mere bodies, but rather our bodies as no less than the whole person made in the image of God. Body and spirit are not two independent realities, as so many modern people—including many Christians— believe, but rather together constitute the one person. Thus our bodies are no less destined for eternal life than what we call spirit (or soul). O'Connor was acutely aware that the vast majority of people for whom she was writing lacked this vision of the body. What's more, they failed to see life as transfigured by the action of grace in the material order. That is why in "Novelist and Believer" she maintains that the Christian writer must reject the influence "of those Manichean-type theologies which . . . [see] the natural world as unworthy of penetration." That is because "he knows that the infinite cannot be approached directly" but only in and through the body and the material creation. She concludes that the Christian writer must show in his art, therefore, that grace "penetrate[s] the natural human world as it is," concrete and embodied.[5]

God in Christ became a human being, wholly and not in part, not just mind or soul but also body. The only begotten Son, equal in divinity to the Father, became flesh and was raised from death in his humanity, taking his transfigured body with him to the Father. That is why Christians have looked forward to eternal life, as transfigured bodily life and not a disincarnate existence. In the words of the ancient Athanasian Creed: "All men shall rise again with their bodies. . . . And they that have done good shall go into life everlasting."

O'Connor believed wholly in this dogma and understood that this affirmation of the eternal worth of the body is at the heart of the Christian concept of the dignity of the human person. She agrees with the ancient Christian tradition that the body is the seat and subject of grace and sanctification in the human being. We are temples of the Holy Spirit, bound for transfigured life as Peter, James, and John saw on Mount Tabor, and as the disciples encountered in the Risen Lord.

"The Enduring Chill": The education of a modern gnostic

In "The Enduring Chill," Asbury Fox is a young man filled with hubris and immersed in self-delusion about his talents as a writer. He rejects the Christian religion because he thinks it stands in the way of his artistic imagination and fulfillment as a writer. He says to a priest in the story, "God is an idea created by man," and "The artist prays by creating."[6] Asbury leaves his home on a country farm to live in New York City (the secular city) to make his mark on the literary world. But things do not go well for Asbury. He is not productive and he becomes ill.

His sickness weakens him so that he has no recourse but to return home to what he imagines will be his speedy demise. His sister Mary George, a principal of an elementary school and someone equally smitten with intellectual pride, sarcastically diagnoses Asbury's condition: "Asbury can't write so he gets sick,"[7] she quips. But Asbury's sickness is not just in his head. It is also genuinely physical. Later in the story, we learn that before leaving for the city Asbury drank unpasteurized milk at the family farm in an unsuccessful attempt to make friends with two of the Negro hired hands. From this he contracts undulant fever, called bangs in cows, which causes painfully alternating chills and fevers in humans but is not fatal.

Asbury is one of O'Connor's modern gnostics, alienated from home and his own body, sick with the sin of pride (especially, in his case, intellectual hubris), and attracted to the sort of mysticism that projects man as his own savior and perfecter. Since childhood, Asbury has resisted that grace which is neither of his own conjuring nor in service to his selfish ways. A water stain on the ceiling above his bed is the sign of this grace which he resists. For as long as Asbury can remember, it has been there, taking the form of a fierce bird with icicles in its claws making ready to descend on him. At the close of the story, Asbury lies in bed dreadfully sick but also aware that he is not going to die. "The old life in him [is] exhausted [and] a new is about to be born, [as] the bird appear[s] all at once in motion," and descends. O'Connor announces, "It is the Holy Ghost emblazoned in ice instead of fire."[8]

"The Enduring Chill" is as complex a story as Flannery O'Connor penned, and I cannot touch on all facets of its meaning. Several details in the story, however, point to its principal themes. Early on, O'Connor establishes that Asbury has a "peculiar" relationship to the bovine species. It is not just that he drinks their milk and gets sick. More important is the fact that although he is not a cow, he *can* get sick with a disease that *is* a cow disease. O'Connor reminds us that human beings share an animal nature with other creatures. During a car ride back to the farm, Asbury notices that "a small walleyed Guernsey . . . [is] watching him steadily as if she sense[s] some bond between them." With sardonic humor, O'Connor comments: "On the point of death, he found himself existing in a state of illumination that was totally out of keeping with the kind of talk he had to listen to from his mother. This was largely about cows with names like Daisy and Bessie Button and their intimate functions—their mastisis and their screw-worms and their abortions."[9]

Asbury's endeavors to practice an intellectual angelism meet defeat. He wants to die, or more accurately, he wants to shed his body even if it means his dying. His disease-wracked body, his mother, the cows—all remind him of everything that he detests about his life, all prevent him from achieving his great artistic work. But his "illumination" is not prevented by his body, the presence of his mother, or the cows. Rather, his egocentrism, intellectual hubris, and self-imposed removal from everyday life are the causes of his creative block. "No art is sunk in the self, but rather, in art the self becomes self-forgetful in order to meet the demands of the thing seen and the thing being made," says O'Connor in one of her essays. "I think it is usually some form of self-inflation that destroys the free use of a gift."[10] Ironically, the bird that descends on Asbury is a product of his (until now caged) furtive imagination, suggesting that his most creative period might lie ahead of him. Asbury will go on living his embodied existence. Properly humbled, he might even inherit the kingdom of God, because "the last film of illusion . . . [has been] torn as if by a whirlwind from his eyes."[11]

"Parker's Back": The tattooed Christ

Like the Christian humanism of the past, Flannery O'Connor's humanism is grounded in an unwavering incarnational faith and sacramental vision of creation. Faced with the modern temper, she chose a strategy that she gambled would shake the spiritual cataracts from her secular readers' eyes and open their vision to the operations of grace in the everyday world. It is fitting that one of her last stories is arguably her most profound affirmation of this incarnational and sacramental vision of human nature and destiny.

O'Connor completed "Parker's Back" in her hospital bed in defiance of her doctor's instructions not to press her own failing body any further. The story is the crowning achievement of O'Connor's Christian humanism. In it, she resoundingly rejects and rebuts the gnostic impulses of the culture. Her instrument is a tragicomic country character who shows— by what he feels and does more than by what he thinks—that the complete man, the truly fulfilled human being, "incarnates" God in his life, and in so doing inherits Paradise.

Obadiah Elihue Parker is the opposite of Asbury Fox in almost every respect, except that like Asbury he is driven by a desire for perfection. Asbury is an intellectual who thinks he can create truth and beauty out of his own head; whereas Parker—for that is the name he goes by, since he is ashamed of his first and middle names—wants to wear beauty on his body. When O'Connor introduces us to him at the beginning of the story, Parker is twenty-eight years old and has married a young woman named Sarah Ruth, the daughter of a fundamentalist preacher. "They were married in the County Ordinary's office because Sarah Ruth thought churches were idolatrous."[12]

Parker's life was changed forever when he was fourteen years old. That was when, at the fair, he set his eyes on the man whose entire body, from head to foot, was covered with tattoos. "Until he saw that man," O'Connor writes, "it did not enter his head that there was anything out of the ordinary about the fact of his existence."[13] In this unlikely place, on the body of this sideshow freak, Parker discovers mystery. Unlike Asbury, he has no words to express his discovery, but a burning desire for beauty is born within him. "The man who was small and sturdy, moved on the platform, flexing his muscles so that the arabesque of men and beasts and flowers on his skin appeared to have a subtle motion of its own."[14] Without really being conscious of it, Parker is headed in a new direction. "It was as if a blind boy had been turned so gently in a different direction that he did not know his destination had been changed."[15]

From the moment he saw the tattooed man, Parker wanted to wear nothing but bright colors and beautiful designs. He began to acquire tattoos. But, strangely, no tattoo satisfied him for very long; and "as the space on the front of him for tattoos decreased, his dissatisfaction grew and became general." No combination seemed to achieve the desired result. The overall effect was not the harmony of color, form, and movement that Parker had seen on the tattooed man, but "something haphazard and botched."[16] Though unable to articulate it, Parker had discovered the profound truth that the human person is a microcosm of the creation—that in man, whom God created in his own image, the whole universe reverberates and strives toward redemption. This truth is reflected in Parker's own eyes, which are "the same pale slate-color as the ocean and reflect the immense spaces around him as if they were the microcosm of the mysterious sea."[17]

Parker is eventually left with but one space on his body to fill: his back. He wants to please his wife, who is displeased with virtually everything he says, does, or owns, including—most especially—his tattoos. But even though she abhors them, Parker is convinced that the right tattoo will win Sarah Ruth's approval. "He visualized having a tattoo put [on his back] that Sarah Ruth would not be able to resist—a religious subject. He thought of an open book with HOLY BIBLE tattooed under it and an actual verse printed on the page. This seemed just the thing for a while; then he began to hear her say, 'Ain't I got a real Bible? What you think I want to read the same verse over and over for when I can read it all?' He needed something even better."[18]

One day, Parker crashes a tractor into a tree and sets the tree on fire. Like Moses before the burning bush, he has a revelation. "All at once he saw the tree reaching out to grasp him: a ferocious thud propelled him into the air, and he heard himself yelling in an unbelievably loud voice, 'GOD ABOVE!' . . . He landed on his back while the tractor crashed up-side down into the tree and burst into flame. . . . He scrambled backwards, still sitting, his eyes cavernous, and if he had known how to cross himself he would have done it."[19] Immediately, Parker sets off in his truck from the scene of his epiphany to the city, where he visits the local tattoo artist. Parker is now certain that nothing short of a tattoo of God himself will please Sarah Ruth. He pages through a book of pictures of God and is stopped by the "all-demanding eyes" of a haloed, flat, stern head of a Byz-antine Christ. It is as if Parker "were being brought to life by a subtle power,"[20] and he decides that this is the image he will have tattooed on his back. The symbolism is rich, reflecting O'Connor's own incarnational and iconographic imagination. Parker has himself inscribed with the image of he who is called the "express image" (Hebrews 1:3) of God the Father, the archetype of our humanity. He dedicates this last remaining space on his body to God.

When Parker arrives at home just before dawn, he uncovers his back and shows Sarah Ruth the tattooed icon. But this does not earn the ex-pected approval. At first Sarah Ruth is confused. She does not recognize the face on his back. "It ain't no body I know," she says. Her words are packed with irony.

"It's him," Parker said.

"Him who?"

"God!" Parker cried.

"God? God don't look like that!"

"What do you know how he looks?" Parker moaned. "You ain't seen him."

"He don't *look*," Sarah Ruth said. "He's a spirit. No man shall see his face."

"Aw listen," Parker groaned, "this is just a picture of him."

"Idolatry," Sarah Ruth screamed. "Idolatry.... I don't want no idolater in this house!" And she grabbed up the broom and began to thrash him across the shoulders with it. ... [A]nd large welts ... formed on the face of the tattooed Christ. Then he staggered up and made for the door.... Still gripping [the broom], she looked toward the pecan tree and her eyes hardened still more. There he was ... leaning against the tree, crying like a baby.[21]

The story ends here. O'Connor gives it no full closure. The fate of this scourged and "crucified" figure is left unknown. But just before revealing the image of God to his wife, Parker had felt "the light pouring through him, turning his spider web soul into a perfect arabesque of colors, a garden of trees and birds and beasts." Through his search and suffering, Parker had reached the goal of all his yearnings and strivings: he had become the new Adam in Paradise.

Living grand and incarnate lives

In her discussion of "Parker's Back" in *Voice of the Peacock*, Kathleen Feeley comments that it "seems strangely fitting that the story of a man led in mysterious ways to incarnate the Redeemer on his own body should be the final story of an author led by equally mysterious ways to make Redemption a reality in her fiction."[22] Feeley turns our attention back to the powerful incarnational vision that drove Flannery O'Connor's fiction and stood at the heart of her Christian humanism.

O'Connor's iconographic fiction was a response to the gnostic challenges to Christian orthodoxy, challenges she felt compelled to answer. And in "Parker's Back" she helps us to understand where and on what grounds she parts company with the fundamentalist religion of the South—a religion that on various occasions O'Connor, as a Roman Catholic, sided with against secular humanism and liberal Protestantism. As she wrote to Ted R. Spivey, a professor of English at Georgia State University, "[T]he fundamentalist Protestants, as far as doctrine goes, are closer to their traditional enemy, the Church of Rome, than they are to advanced [liberal] elements in Protestantism."[23]

Yet modern fundamentalism doesn't take the Incarnation seriously enough. It limits the limitless God to the written word and denies his presence in the physical creation. Sarah Ruth completely fails to detect God's presence in the drama that unfolds around her. She is unable to see the image of God in her husband and does not comprehend his participation in the suffering of Christ and his redemptive victory on the cross. Could this be because she is a modern Christian gnostic? O'Connor leaves Sarah Ruth no better off in relation to God and humanity than the secular people she abhors.

On another occasion, Flannery O'Connor penned these words about her art, words that crystallize in her characteristically homespun way her remarkable vision. "Fiction," she wrote, "is about everything human and we are made out of dust, and if you scorn getting yourself dusty, then you shouldn't try to write fiction. It's not a grand enough job for you."[24] That piece of wisdom is applicable not just to writing, but to the whole of living.

Rallying the Human things: by Gurdian Vigen

irk:

and Conservatism

ion with Russell and Annette Kirk ...Washington, D.C., just five months before Dr. Kirk's death, Russell turned to me and quipped, with his familiar chuckle and impish smile, "Vigen, they are now calling me a theologian!" I did not ask him who was saying such a thing. I realized that he was speaking only half seriously and with ironic intent. Yet if, for instance, one examines *Redeeming the Time,* a superior collection of some of Russell Kirk's later lectures and essays, it certainly appears that matters theological had begun to occupy an increasing portion of his mind.

The lead essay in *Redeeming the Time* poses a question: "Civilization without Religion?" The answer Kirk gives is that a civilization in which the religious cult has withered will not survive. "What ails modern civilization? Fundamentally, our society's affliction is the decay of religious belief," Kirk writes. "If the culture is to survive and flourish, it must not be severed from the religious vision out of which it arose." Of course, there are those who seem to desire nothing so much as that very severance, which is why it is so important that "reflective men and women . . . labor for the restoration of religious teachings as a credible body of doctrine."[1]

The final essay in *Redeeming the Time* is titled "The Wise Men Know What Wicked Things Are Written on The Sky." This line is from G. K. Chesterton's epic poem "The Ballad of the White Horse." Chesterton biographer Maisie Ward explains that the poem honors "Christian men, whether they be Saxon or Roman or Briton or Celt, . . . banded together to fight the heathen Danes in defence of the sacred things of faith, in defence of the human things of daily life, in defence even of the old traditions of pagan England, . . . 'because it is only Christian men / guard even heathen things.'"[2]

Most of Kirk's interpreters have failed to dig deeply into his views on religion and culture. This failure might be explained by the fact that most commentators have been interested in his political thought: Kirk on conservatism, Kirk on natural law, Kirk on the American Constitution, and so forth. Yet Kirk often stated his belief that political questions are rooted in matters of morality, and that both of these, in turn, are grounded, explicitly or implicitly, in religious faith.

In fact, Kirk did not think of himself chiefly as a political thinker. It is also true, as Kirk indicated at our dinner that evening, that he was no theologian. I am convinced, however, that he was pleased when he chortled about some people having noticed the degree to which his thought was theologically informed. For faith is a presupposition of most everything that Russell Kirk wrote and said about politics or the good commonwealth. Kirk may not have been a theologian, but he took religion seriously. What is more, from first to last he expressed great admiration and respect for the long and venerable tradition of Christian humanism, a tradition with which he identified strongly. In this chapter, I argue that Russell Kirk himself exemplified this tradition, and that its influence on his thought was definitive.

Kirk the Christian humanist

In *The Sword of Imagination,* his posthumously published autobiography, Kirk states that humanism in just "one form—that of Erasmus and More—did enrich Christianity."[3] This is no late judgment, however. In an article written in the 1950s, titled "Pico Della Mirandola and Human Dignity," Kirk observes that the best of the Renaissance Christian humanists, among them Pico, believed that "for human dignity to exist, there must be a Master who can raise man above the brute creation. If the Master is denied, then dignity for man is unattainable."[4] "For all his glorification of Man," Kirk adds, Pico, and men such as Thomas More and Erasmus, did not believe, as do the modern secular humanists, that "man makes himself.... [Rather,] it is only because man was created in the image of God that man is almost angelic."[5]

In other words, these great Christian humanists believed that man is a theonomous being, which is to say that God has revealed the fullness and perfection of our human nature in the God-man, Jesus Christ, who is himself, according to Saint Paul, "the image of the invisible God, the first born of all creation" (Colossians 1:15). The dignity of the human being is grounded in the *imago Dei,* which God has given to humankind through his creative act. With the use of his rational and spiritual powers, man can aspire "to struggle upward toward the Godhead." Yet the Renaissance humanists did not believe that this perfection (sanctification) in the image of God was inevitable or that it obeyed some law of progress or evolution. Pico and those like him understood that by misusing these very same powers man is capable of denying and degrading the image of God within him and sinking "to the level of the brutes."[6]

Like the Renaissance or Christian humanists, modern secular humanism propounds, often, a doctrine of the dignity of man, but unlike the former, secular humanism attributes this dignity solely to human reason and autonomy. It rejects the Christian vision of theonomous man, whose dignity comes from the God who created him in his image and who has entered into a covenantal relationship with man to secure his salvation from a fallen estate.

Ironically, because of its very supposition of human autonomy, secular humanism degrades humankind. Kirk observes:

> Despite all the cant concerning the dignity of man in our time, the real tendency of recent intellectual currents has been to sweep true human dignity down to a morass of mechanistic indignity. Joseph Wood Krutch, a generation ago, in his *Modern Temper*, described with a somber resignation this process of degradation. Without God, man cannot aspire to rank with the cherubim and seraphim. Freud convinced the crowd of intellectuals that man was nothing better than the slave of obscure and arrogant fleshly desires; Alfred Kinsey, unintentionally reducing to absurdity this denial of human dignity, advised his fellow-creatures to emulate, if not the ant, at least the snake—for man, so the modern dogma goes, lives only to lust. In this fashion phrases [like the dignity of the person] linger in men's mouths long after the object they describe has been forgotten.[7]

Kirk closes "Pico Della Mirandola and Human Dignity" by quoting Emerson:

> There are two laws discrete
> Not reconciled,—
> Law for man, and law for thing;
> The last builds town and fleet,
> But it runs wild,
> And doth the man unking.[8]

Kirk comments that in our day, the "law for thing" rules. Modern man's remarkable inventions and technology possess enormous potential to enhance human life and relieve human suffering. Yet these powers can subvert human dignity and cheapen life if man views himself in purely instrumental terms. Just "when man's power over nature is at its summit,"[9] he seems bent on "unkinging" himself, says Kirk. For instance, the biotechnological revolution is filled with the promise of wonderful preventative and curative medicine. Hubris and impiety, however, move modern man to tamper radically with the human gene pool and to treat individual life as a commodity and disposable good—this whether one is speaking of abortion, physician-assisted suicide, embryonic stem-cell research, or various reproductive technologies, including cloning. Denial, explicit or implicit, of the divine image in the human person lies at the heart of modern nihilism, says Kirk. Modern man not only commits deicide in his heart and mind but homicide with his hands and machines.

The Renaissance humanists admired the philosophy, literature, and art of classical Greece and Rome. They endeavored to reclaim for their contemporaries this treasury of antiquity's wisdom while remaining guided by the light of the Christian Gospel. They believed in the essential goodness of man and God's intention to redeem each and every human being. But they were also acutely aware of human foible and sin. Therefore, they especially valued humility in personal conduct and magnanimity in public life. They were confident that God respects and will not contravene human freedom. Thus, they encouraged their contemporaries to endeavor "through moral disciplines of *humanitas*, ... to struggle upward toward the Godhead."[10] Kirk recommends that we revisit the wisdom of these humanists, as it may assist us in our crucial struggle with the dangerously dehumanizing forces let loose by modernity.

Over the years, Kirk enumerated a list of writers and thinkers whom he credited with transmitting and deepening this tradition of Christian humanism. Included on this list were Richard Hooker, Edmund Burke, John Henry Newman, Orestes Brownson, G. K. Chesterton, Christopher

Dawson, and T. S. Eliot, among others. For instance, in *The Sword of Imagi-nation* Kirk recalls that during his study of Burke in the late 1940s he was drawn to "Richard Hooker and other great Anglican divines," and that John Henry Newman became his principal instructor in classical dog-matic Christianity.[11]

Kirk, who entered into the Roman Catholic Church in 1964, believed in the personal God of Christian orthodoxy. His God was not merely the First Cause or Prime Mover of which the philosophers speak. Nor was he myth, symbol, or cipher for human self-transcendence. Kirk's God is the triune divinity of the Father, the Son, and the Holy Spirit, the God who reveals himself to the whole of humankind through the Incarnation of the Son and through the church that is his Body. In an interview excerpted by William F. Buckley Jr. in *Nearer, My God*, Kirk states that lacking "the Res-urrection . . . , what we call Christianity would be a mere congeries of moral exhortations, at best. The Resurrection in the flesh . . . proved that indeed Jesus the Son had transcended matter and was divine. . . . [His] Resurrection . . . prefigures our own resurrection and life everlasting."[12]

The tales Kirk told

Russell Kirk's Christian humanism is as specific and particular as this con-fession of faith.[13] Nowhere, perhaps, is this more evident than in the gothic ghost stories that he wrote, which he described as "experiments in the moral imagination."[14] These are not typically modern tales of the occult. They are about divine judgment, forgiveness, and redemption. Through character and plot, Kirk illumines how the grace of God works in and penetrates through the whole fabric of human existence, indeed, the whole created order.

The early tales, written during the 1950s and '60s, are noteworthy for their acerbic criticism of political rationalism and government-sponsored social engineering projects. Kirk gives us petty bureaucrats and government agents who, with unflinching and sometimes maniacal faith in technology and progress, threaten to bring grave harm to the complex ecology of human life. Without the slightest regret, they are intent upon ripping up the precious fabric of traditional community and old habits of life.

The story "Ex Tenebris" portrays S. G. W. Barner, Planning Officer, an arrogant and willful official who "has made up his mind that not one stone was to be left upon another at Low Wentford. With satisfaction he had seen the last of the farm-laborers of the hamlet transferred to the new council-houses at Gorst, where there was no lack of communal facilities, including six cinemas."[15] There is no room in Barner's plan for Low Wentford's old and abandoned fifteenth-century church, All Saints. "No church had yet been erected in the newest housing scheme at Gorst: Cultural amenities must yield pride of place to material requirements, Barner had declared."[16] The old church is emblematic of the spiritual reality to which human beings belong and upon which they depend for lasting meaning in their lives. If human beings ignore or reject that reality, they invite grave ill and suffering upon themselves.

Moved by a utilitarian, atheistic spirit, S. G. W. Barner callously uproots the lives of ordinary people. But as with other characters in Kirk's stories, Barner runs up against a ghostly avenger and executor of divine judgment. The tormented spirit of a former vicar of the parish, one Reverend Abner Hargreaves, lures Barner one evening to the abandoned church. The weather has turned raw and rainy, and Barner suggests that the two take shelter in the church. "Safe in the church?" the vicar responds. "You and I? Never!" And Hargreaves grabs "Barner by the throat."[17] The next day, Barner's crushed corpse is found beneath the collapsed roof of the north porch. For the time being, at least, Low Wentford is spared. "The county council has relinquished the scheme for clearing the site of Low Wentford, indeed there appears to be some possibility that six or seven of the cottages near the bridge may be restored. . . . Mrs. Oliver's cottage, in any event seems secure. She weeds her garden and bakes her scones, and often sweeps the gravestones clean."[18]

In his later stories of the 1970s and 1980s, Kirk becomes increasingly concerned with theological and mystical themes of time and eternity. He also asks his readers to consider what constitutes a life worthy of God's favor and redemption. In these stories, Kirk deepens his Christian anthropology. Every human being, man and woman, is created in the image and likeness of God. Yet because sin corrupts human freedom, reason, and imagination, the struggle between good and evil that occurs in each individual heart is externalized into society and its institutions.

Through such heroes as Frank Sarsfield of "There's a Long, Long Trail A-Winding," Father Raymond Thomas Montrose of "The Invasion of the Church of the Holy Ghost," and Ian Inchburn of "The Reflex-Man in Whinnymuir Close," Kirk convincingly, sometimes shockingly, makes his case about this struggle of good and evil. And he demonstrates that nothing less than eternal life lies in the balance. Thus, despite his having succeeded in not falling to the worst temptations of lust and violence, or perhaps just because of that, Fr. Raymond Thomas Montrose makes this moving penance at the close of "The Invasion of the Church of the Holy Ghost": "In all of us sinners the flesh is weak; and the future, unknowable, has its many corridors and issues. . . . Puffed up with pride of spirit, by which fault fell angels, I came near to serving the Prince of the Air. From the ravenous powers of darkness, O Lord, let me be preserved."[19]

Kirk frequently employs T. S. Eliot's images of the Wasteland in his fiction. The terrain that Kirk's characters inhabit is strewn with the faded images and broken objects of our civilization, shards of the past that once constituted a uniform culture informed by a vital Christian faith. This terrain is vividly portrayed in the opening scenes of "There's a Long, Long Trail A-Winding":

Along the vast empty six-lane highway, the blizzard swept as if it meant to swallow all the sensual world. Frank Sarsfield, massive though he was, scudded like a heavy kite before that overwhelming wind. . . . He had walked thirty miles that day

.... This was depopulated country, its forests gone to the sawmills long before, its mines worked out. The freeway ran through the abomination of desolation.... The village was more distant than he had thought.... A little to the west he noticed what seemed to be old mine-workings, with fragments of brick buildings. He clambered upon an old railroad bed, its rails and ties taken up; perhaps the new freeway had dealt the final blow to the rails.[20]

Like the sojourner-seeker of T. S. Eliot's famous poem, Sarsfield comes upon a ruined church, once again emblematic of a land and people that are spiritually desolate.

Anthonyville Free Methodist Church hulked before him. Indeed the bell was swinging, and now and again faintly ringing in the steeple; but it was the wind's mockery, a knell for the derelict town of Anthonyville. The church door was slamming in the high wind, ... the glass being gone from the church windows. Sarsfield trudged past the skeletal church.[21]

The decay and despair, the violence and destruction, the brokenness and barrenness of modern life are not merely external to the self, however. The Wasteland exists inside of us as well. It is our total environment, deadly not only to our bodies, but more importantly to our souls.

The task of Christian humanism

The entire body of Kirk's work, fiction and nonfiction alike, alerts us to the fact that our culture is in the midst of a crisis which is eviscerating meaning and dehumanizing life. Yet Kirk was no despairing cynic. He thought it possible that a restatement of Christian orthodoxy could effect cultural recovery. "Given imagination," he announces in "The Wise Men Know What Wicked Things Are Written on the Sky,"

> Americans may refute the prophesies of decadence. Whether those wicked things on the sky will be erased in the age that is dawning, or whether the children of darkness prevail—why, that will be decided by the rising generation, in whose power it will be to give the lie to fatalists. . . . Providence, it seems, is quite often as retributory as it is beneficent, and ordinarily Providence operates through human agency. In the hope of moving the thoughts and sentiments of some few people . . . for the renewal of moral and political order—why, in that hope these lectures were delivered.[22]

Kirk recognized that, in an earlier age, the pressing requirements of justice and timely reform, both within the church and the political order, had moved Dante, Erasmus, and More to articulate their Christian humanism. Erasmus and More reacted to a dry and desiccating Scholasticism. They propounded a philosophy and social criticism that returned the focus of faith onto the human person in his or her freedom and creativity. In contrast to the utopianism of modern social radicals, however, all three of these great Christians understood the difference between a reform that conserves and replenishes and an innovation that tears down in pursuit of private fantasy. As Kirk writes:

> Never deluded, the Christian humanist . . . does not despise the past simply because it is old, nor does he assume that the present is delightful simply because it is ours. He judges every age and every institution in the light of certain principles of justice and order, which we have learned in part through revelation and in part through the long and painful experience of the human race. When the Christian humanist says that

much is wrong with our time, that it is out of joint, he does not mean that things ever were ordered perfectly, in all respects, in some past epoch; nor does he have a vision of a future society in which all the imperfections of human nature will be wiped away, and all desires perfectly satisfied. He can be historically eclectic; he may approve this feature of another age, and disapprove a great deal in any period.[23]

In *Rights and Duties: Reflections on Our Conservative Constitution*, Kirk claims: "Secular humanism is a creed or world view that holds we have no reason to believe in a creator; that the world is 'self-existing'; that no transcendent power is at work in the world; that we should not turn to traditional religion for wisdom, but rather we should develop a new ethics or method of moral science."[24] And in "Pico," Kirk concludes: "If Things are to be thrust out of the saddle once more, and Man mounted (in Pico's phrase) 'to join battle as to the sound of a trumpet of war' on behalf of man's higher nature, then some of us must go barefoot through the world, like Pico, preaching the vegetative and sensual errors of our time."[25]

It is difficult to imagine Russell Kirk traipsing barefoot anywhere—Kirk's hiking boots were always at the ready. But whether barefoot or booted, Kirk relentlessly exposed "the vegetative and sensual errors of our time." He understood deeply that the West owes its respect for the sacredness of human life to biblical religion and Christianity in particular. In this respect, the term "Christian humanism" is a redundancy. Christianity *is* belief in a God who has become a *human being,* and by his resurrection from the dead *has shown and affirmed* that every human person is of eternal worth. Jesus Christ is not just lawgiver, judge, or moral exemplar. When the Christian religion is reduced to fundamentalism, legalism, or moralism, even it might be turned into an instrument that destroys human personality and denies human freedom.

Christian humanism versus secular humanism

Russell Kirk was aware that others had also claimed the mantel of humanism, but in the name of secularism. The revival of Christian humanism in our time is spurred by the need to respond to the rise of this popular secular humanism and its half-truths. The philosopher and educator John Dewey was one of this ideology's most ardent proponents. In his misnamed "Religious Humanist Manifesto," Dewey stated that man's animal nature and rational faculties fully accounted for human morality and civilization.[26] He argued that there is nothing "over" or "above" man to which he is related or that must be addressed. Like the Renaissance Christian humanists, Dewey and his followers attached a high value to education. But they believed that the methods and aims of modern education must be strictly rational and instrumental, aimed at developing skills of social intercourse and productivity that promote a just and harmonious secular realm. Education must not refer to anything transcendent nor be founded in moral or religious certitude.

It is easy to understand why Kirk opposed this sort of secular humanism. Even an agnostic, perhaps relying on some form of natural law philosophy, might well subscribe to a normative view of human nature and stand against relativism. But Kirk was not satisfied with such a position—and the reasons why are important to the thesis I have been pursuing.

In *A Program for Conservatives* (later reissued as *Prospects for Conservatives*), Kirk insists, "The true conservative, in the tradition of Burke or of Adams, is a theist, for he sees this world as a place of trial, governed by a power beyond human ability to completely comprehend adequately."[27] And in the first edition of his seminal work, *The Conservative Mind*, Kirk lists six canons of conservatism, the first of which is unabashedly religious. Conservatism, he maintains, is established on the "belief that a divine intent rules society as well as conscience, forging an eternal chain of duty and right, which links great and obscure, living and dead. Political problems, at bottom, are religious and moral problems."[28]

Yet despite these claims about the relationship between conservatism and theism, Kirk includes in his pantheon of conservatism those who were not theists. One of these is Irving Babbitt, professor of French literature at Harvard from 1894 to 1933. Babbitt inspired and led the New Humanist movement that aroused considerable interest and controversy in America and England during the first four decades of the past century. Kirk discovered Babbitt early in his career. He was deeply impressed by Babbitt's brilliant critiques of liberalism, modern education, and secular humanism. But after serious consideration, Kirk came to reject Babbitt's view that the distinguishing mark of the human animal is the "ethical will," which requires no reference to the divinity.

In *The Conservative Mind* Kirk says little about Babbitt's rejection of theism. Later, however, as he studied the work of T. S. Eliot and other Christian writers such as Christopher Dawson and Martin D'Arcy, Kirk saw fit to address the matter. Eliot had been a student of Babbitt at Harvard, and his criticism of Babbitt was particularly effective in persuading Kirk that this defect in Babbitt's thought was significant.

Babbitt contended that there were two dominant types of secular humanism. The first is the scientistic sort that views technology as a savior that will bring into existence a new age of social justice and human flourishing. The second is the sentimental or Rousseauian variety, which maintains that man is corrupted by traditional society and must liberate himself from it in order to enjoy genuine freedom and happiness. Both, Babbitt rightly argued, are wedded to philosophical naturalism and moral relativism.

Eliot did not quarrel with this typology of secular humanism. But he rejected Babbitt's claim that his so-called ethical humanism negotiated successfully a middle ground between naturalism and supernaturalism, thereby ensuring the dignity of the human person on purely empirical, philosophical grounds. Eliot argued that Babbitt could not have it both ways: he could not affirm human freedom and the ethical will while also rejecting theism. In other words, Babbitt's ethical will is not what distinguishes man from nature and the rest of the animal kingdom, but rather man's relationship to the supernatural. "Man is man because he can recognize supernatural realities, not because he can invent them," wrote Eliot in an essay on the New Humanism. "Either everything in man can be traced as a development from below," from an essentially closed system we call nature, "or something must come from above,"[29] from a source that transcends the bounds of that system and may even have brought it into being.

Thus, either man is explicable in terms of a self-existent total system that needs no God—the view of naturalism—or else human nature can be fully understood only by incorporating an account of humankind's relation to a Divine Reality (or a Supreme Being). If it really is possible to fully explain human existence in terms of nature, then neither the freedom nor the morality Babbitt defended really exists, since every human thought and action is, in theory, fully explainable within the terms of a determinate series of causes and effects. Nature's "law," seen from a secular and scientific point of view, is necessity, to which freedom is alien. "If you remove from the word 'human' all that the belief in the supernatural has given to man," writes Eliot, "you can view him finally as no more than a clever, adaptable, and mischievous animal."[30]

Eliot did not deny that nature is "in" man and that man is "in" nature. But he insisted that this does not exclude the possibility that supernature is also "in" man and man "in" it. Nature (or Creation) is not some "thing" upon which God acts from without; rather, God expresses himself "in" and "through" nature. The human being is the supreme example of God's "indwelling" in nature, since God himself became human, just as he created humankind in his own image. That is why human existence genuinely transcends the necessity and determinacy of the "nature" proposed by secular humanism. The existence of the biblical God posits both divine and human freedom.

Kirk wrote a lengthy introduction to a new edition of Babbitt's *Literature and the American College*, issued in 1987. In that introduction he favorably summarizes Eliot's criticism of Babbitt. "Eliot's argument is that Babbitt, like nearly all twentieth-century writers of Protestant or even Protestant-agnostic background, has rejected the religion of his childhood but has not acquired other theological and moral premises for his writings."[31] "The Christian humanism of Erasmus and Sir Thomas More clearly was a source of Babbitt's own humanism,"[32] but his rejection of the "religious assumptions about the human condition" to which these humanists also held "starves" the very "moral imagination" that Babbitt wanted to defend.[33] Babbitt left open the gates to moral relativism, despite his heroic efforts to close them and hold back the tide of secularism.

Kirk therefore judges Eliot's view of Babbitt's thought to be "just." Babbitt "said that economics moves upward into politics, and politics upwards into ethics; but on whether ethics moves upwards into theology, he was equivocal." For whatever reason, "Babbitt refused to proceed beyond 'tradition' to the religious sources of tradition."[34] And this refusal left his philosophy deeply flawed.

Russell Kirk believed that only biblical theism is capable of combating relativism and renewing our culture. His theistic conservatism was a form of Christian humanism. Perhaps the most revealing evidence of Kirk's strong identification with this great Christian tradition appears in his discussion of Eliot's beliefs concerning Babbitt. In *Eliot and His Age*, Kirk writes that Babbitt's "humanism . . . stung Eliot as if it had been a gadfly, rousing curiosity and inquiry; his reaction, after his leaving Harvard, was a gradual transcending of the humanist argument, a fulfillment rather than a rejection of Babbitt's teaching. Like Thomas More and Erasmus, Eliot became both humanist and Christian."[35] Kirk could not have offered any greater praise for Eliot than this, precisely because Kirk himself had found and embraced the same good company.

· 2 ·

On the
Moral Imagination

4

On Fairy Tales and

the Moral Imagination

I am a gardener, so I know that the good essay on gardening pays attention to the characteristics and habits of weeds. This chapter on the moral imagination, therefore, pays attention to some of the worst and most unholy forms of imagination, forms that spread like weeds in an ill-kept flower garden and choke out the best cultivars.

Too many people naïvely associate the imagination solely or even primarily with what is moral and good. Keats went too far when he rhapsodized: "I am certain of nothing but the holiness of the heart's affections and the truth of imagination—what the imagination seizes as beauty must be truth." The human heart's desires may not be holy, and the imagination born of these unholy desires may even be demonic. After all, it was the tyrant Napoleon who hauntingly declared, "Imagination rules the world."

The Book of Proverbs declares, "Where there is no vision, the people perish" (29:18). Where there is no real moral imagination, itself a form of vision, the people will become captives of corrupt and corrupting forms of imagination, for while imagination as such may be an innate human capacity, it needs proper nurture and cultivation. If the tea rose is not properly attended it withers and the thistle grows in its place. If the moral imagination is not fed by religious sentiment and supported by reason, it will wither and be replaced by corrupt forms of imagination.

Thus, I need to name and describe three forms of imagination that flourish in the garden of our society, weeds that are crowding out the flowering of the moral imagination. These I am calling the idyllic imagination, the idolatrous imagination, and the diabolic imagination.

Stories we live by

Our society is failing to cultivate the moral imagination because very often the stories we live by—the stories we read ourselves or read to our children, the stories we watch on television or at the movies—are not stories that grow the moral imagination, but stories that crowd it out. Others have testified to the lively manner in which the traditional myths and fairy tales feed and nurture the moral imagination, especially in the young—but not exclusively the young, for they were invented for the entertainment and edification of adults.

In *Enemies of the Permanent Things*, Russell Kirk reminded us that "[t]he story of Pandora, or Thor's adventure with the old woman and her cat, gives any child insight into the conditions of existence, dimly grasped at the moment, perhaps, but gaining in power as the years pass, that no utilitarian 'real life situation' fiction can match." The process wherein imagination illuminates reason, wrote Kirk, by which it provides sight and insight, "that illative sense described by John Henry Newman—that valid if complex means of normative judgment produced by the conjunction of a great variety of little proofs, illustrations, and inferences, sense—is developed early in life, in no small part, by the wisdom latent in traditional fantasy."

The telling and reading of such stories is "a natural activity," J. R. R. Tolkien noted in his famous essay "On Fairy-Stories."

> It certainly does not destroy or even insult Reason; and it does not either blunt the appetite for, nor obscure the perception of, scientific verity. . . . For creative fantasy is founded upon the hard recognition that things are so in the world as it appears under the sun, on the recognition of fact, *but not slavery to it* [my emphasis]. . . . If men could not distinguish between frogs and men, fairy-tales about frog-kings would not arise.

Children find frog-princes interesting because they see themselves as incomplete, as not entirely whole. They are attracted to the story of "The Ugly Duckling" or "The Little Lame Prince" because reason tells them, based upon simple observation, that they too are in some sense ugly or lame with respect to adults. When they long for the day when they are equal in strength and capacity to grown-ups, the imagination comes into its own.

Children want to explore just what it might be like to finally turn out "whole" and all right, to be a good child, a good parent, or the best of rulers. Pinocchio is the quintessential child. This yearning to be whole and wholly real attracts even adults to fairy kings and queens, to Prince Caspian in C. S. Lewis's *Narnia Chronicles* or Princess Irene of George MacDonald's *The Princess and the Goblin*, because reason and observation tell them that they are ugly, lame, and incomplete with respect to what they might be and were meant to be.

For more than a decade, I have taught a course titled "Religion in Children's Literature." Each year, the young men and women in this class say that in their childhood they were deprived of these resources of the moral imagination. They were not introduced to most of the stories and books on the syllabus and their natural sense of wonder was starved.

I don't have to persuade them that the tasty food of fairy tales and the classic children's stories like those I have just mentioned are good for the soul. Books like *Bambi*, *The Secret Garden*, and *The Wind in the Willows*, not to mention the fairy tales of the Brothers Grimm, Hans Christian Andersen, and Oscar Wilde, possess a richness, texture, and elevating quality accessible to anyone who reads them, regardless of age. My students take advantage of these stories to revisit childhood one last time before entering the adult world. It is a wonderfully satisfying experience. They find themselves not only looking back but also forward to their futures.

Interestingly, my students especially enjoy James Barrie's *Peter Pan* and the Mowgli stories in Rudyard Kipling's *Jungle Books*, since these tales concern two children who don't want to grow up. They are fascinated by the way in which these stories dramatize the role of freedom in human development, its right use and its wrong use. The correct exercise of freedom, they learn, perfects the virtues, while the misuse of freedom leads to vicious habits and destructive behavior.

The stories of Peter and Mowgli end in different ways. Peter refuses to join the lost boys in the Darling household. He returns to Never Land, where he remains a child and a prisoner of his own passions, though he continues to think he is free. We come to see that his humanity is incomplete and malformed. Even his vivid and fertile imagination, of which we may initially be jealous, is trapped in irresponsible childhood and therefore dangerous to others.

By contrast, the love and wisdom of his animal mentors enable Mowgli to mature as a moral being. He struggles with choices and takes responsible action to protect beasts and human beings whom he loves. His powers of memory, reason, and love grow as he takes responsibility for himself and others under the law of the jungle, and he reenters human society a mature young man.

Imagination's purpose

At the start of the last century, Harvard professor Irving Babbitt wrote on the imagination in his memorable study *Literature and the American College*. The human imagination "reaches out and seizes likenesses and analogies" that establish relation and unity in a world of meaning. In other words, imagination is the self's process of finding direction and purpose in life by making metaphors from remembered experiences to understand present experience. It is not an instinct but an attribute and an expression of our freedom, passion, and reason.

Some may think that the important question is whether imagination is waxing or waning in society. But this is not the issue. Wherever there are human beings imagination exists and is exercised, much as wherever there are spiders, webs are spun. The important question is what kinds of imagination our contemporary culture encourages.

We do not worry that spiders might spin their webs badly or misuse them, because spiders spin their webs from instinct, but human beings exercise their imagination freely. Imagination both expresses and trains the reason and the will. Indeed, it is perfectly correct to say that man *is* every bit as much an imaginative creature as a reasoning one or one that possesses a free will.

I do not doubt that imagination is right at the source of what theologians speak of as the image and likeness of God in man. The philosopher George Santayana, a contemporary of Babbitt's, justly maintained that, indeed, the distinction we often make between "intelligence (or reason) and imagination is ideal" and ultimately not sustainable. This distinction, he argued, derives from our need to locate within ourselves a power and source of authority that will validate our deeply seated yearnings for a unified and meaningful life, what he called "spiritual life."

Yet reason, which serves so well for solving the so-called factual problems and theoretical issues of living, cannot of itself project a vision that infuses meaning and purpose into life. "The eye sees what it has been given to see by concrete circumstance," wrote Flannery O'Connor, but "the imagination reproduces what, by some related gift, it is able to make live."

Life is a dynamic process in which reason and imagination are integrated. Thought based solely in sense demands empirical verification and is unable to attain "satisfying or satisfactory conclusions about the spiritual origins" or ends of human life, said Santayana in *Poetry and Religion*. This is where imagination comes in. For imagination furnishes and supplies to religion and morality "those larger ideas" and images which human beings need in order to envision an encompassing meaning and purpose for their lives.

Santayana continued: "Perceptions do not remain in the mind, as would be suggested by the trite simile of the seal and the wax, passive and changeless," as it were, "until we wear off their sharp edges and ... [they] fade." Rather, "perceptions fall into the brain ... as seeds into a furrow or even as sparks into a keg of powder." Each image, in turn, gives birth to more images, "sometimes slowly and subterraneously, sometimes (when a passionate train is started) with a sudden burst of fancy." This, Santayana maintains, is the genesis of imagination, as its images become resources of reason and inspirations to action.

The moral imagination

If that is the imagination, what is the moral imagination? The eighteenth-century British statesman Edmund Burke first coined the term in his great work *Reflections on the Revolution in France*. Lamenting the ferocity and rapidity with which the French revolutionists were destroying the customs and traditional institutions that preserve civility in society, he exclaimed:

> But now all is to be changed. All the pleasing illusions, which
> made power gentle, and obedience liberal, which harmonized
> the different shades of life, and which, by bland assimilation,

incorporated into politics the sentiments which beautify and soften private society, are to be dissolved by this new conquering empire of light and reason. All the decent drapery of life is to be rudely torn off. All of the superadded ideas, furnished from the wardrobe of a moral imagination, which the heart owns and the understanding ratifies, as necessary to cover the defects of our own naked shivering nature, and to raise it to dignity in our estimation, are to be exploded as ridiculous, absurd, and antiquated fashion.

The moral imagination is the distinctively human power to conceive of men and women as moral beings, that is, as persons, not as things or animals whose value to us is their usefulness. It is the process by which the self makes metaphors out of images recorded by the senses and stored in memory, which then are employed to find and suppose moral correspondences in experience.

The principal offices of life in which society invests and entrusts this care are parent and teacher. Modern educators—a breed with which I am all too familiar—have not been good gardeners of the moral life. In their penchant to treat fact as god, event as illusion, individual as datum, person as chimera, norm as relative value, and human nature as social construct, they leave the moral imagination to perish.

What grows in its place? I have mentioned three corrupted forms of imagination. As is the case with all corruptions, corrupted imagination betrays the integrity of the true form. In our everyday life, these corrupted forms manifest decomposition, not wholeness, and perversity, not normality.

The idyllic imagination

The first in the list is the idyllic imagination, named by Irving Babbitt and discussed by him in his books *Democracy and Leadership* and *Rousseau and Romanticism*. The idyllic imagination, he wrote, is fanciful without check, primitivist, and utopian. The self gripped by the idyllic imagination is escapist, not in the sense that it flees its physical surroundings so much as it shirks its civic, social, and moral responsibilities.

This is accompanied and reinforced by rejection and rebellion against old dogmas, manners, and mores. The idyllic imagination is in search of emancipation from conventional constraints. In our democratic and individualistic environment, persons justify this "liberation" in the name of self-fulfillment and self-realization, which they believe existing norms and structures inhibit or obstruct. Quite often there is a turning to hedonistic imaginings, flagrant sensuality, and explorations of the "flesh." These are paths that promise happiness but more often than not lead instead to boredom and ennui or, worse, physical and spiritual dissipation.

This is much documented, both in clinical studies and in great works literary texts, such as Tolstoy's *Anna Karenina* and Flaubert's *Madame Bovary*. In Dostoevsky's *Crime and Punishment*, Svidrigaylov, the middle-aged, dissipated debaucher, sums up this syndrome of the idyllic imagination as he explains to Raskolnikov how he is trapped in a pit of boredom and languor.

> I'll tell you frankly: I'm very bored.... Marfa Petrovna herself
> even suggested twice that I go abroad, seeing I was bored. But
> what for? I used to go abroad, and I always felt sick at heart.
> Nothing special, really—here's the dawn coming up, here's
> the Bay of Naples, the sea—you look, and it's somehow sad.
> The most disgusting thing is that you are always sad about
> something!... I might go on an expedition to the North Pole
> now, because *j'ai le vin mauvais*, drinking disgusts me, and wine
> is the only thing I have left.

During the 1960s, when I came of age, the idyllic imagination flourished in the youth counterculture. It has taken a more troubling turn among college students today, in whom the idealism and utopianism of the sixties is missing, whereas the disillusioning and dissipating symptoms of sensualism and anomie are played out in dormitories and bars.

The idolatrous imagination

The heavy footprints of the second in the trinity of corrupted imaginations may be tracked everywhere in our culture. The media fixes on false gods whose stories replace the lives of saints and real heroes. One need only look at the popular magazines, MTV, talk shows, and celebrity channels to understand how pervasive is the idolatrous imagination.

Even our schools and public libraries are heavily under its influence. I am not talking about movie videos or DVDs only. When I was a boy, books about great scientists, explorers, and statesmen dominated the shelves of the Stark Elementary School library. Today poorly written books about athletes and rock and movie stars have taken their place.

The ancient Hebrews understood the dangers of the idolatrous imagination. Idolatry, in biblical terms, is the giving of one's highest loyalties and devotions to objects and things other than God. Idolatry is "the absolutization of the relative," wrote my mentor and teacher, Will Herberg, in *Judaism and Modern Man*. The object of idolatrous devotion "may be, and in fact generally is, some *good*; but since it is not God, it is necessarily a good that is only partial and relative. What idolatry does is to convert its object into an absolute, thereby destroying the partial good within it and transforming it into a total evil. . . . Idols are both 'vanities' and 'demons.'" Our culture's appropriation and redefinition of a term that once stood for the opposite of idol typifies its forgetfulness of this wisdom. Icons were religious paintings of the saints, who replaced pagan idols by pointing the pious toward the one true God. Today we call our celebrity idols "icons."

Already this sort of religious speech and reasoning is strange and unintelligible to postmodern people. I define a postmodern person quite simply as someone who is almost wholly unfamiliar with biblical faith, whether in contemporaneous or historical form, who, therefore, also lacks a sense of sin. It is next to impossible to persuade such a person that he or she is in thrall to the idolatrous imagination or suffers from the misplaced devotion that idolatry connotes.

When confronted with this kind of speech, such a person is likely to retort: "Well, even if I am in thrall to such an idolatrous imagination, as you say, what harm is it to anyone?" As Herberg rightly observed, "Our modern idolatries, are thus like the Baal practices of the Israelites in Canaan, modes of everyday life rather then explicit confessions of faith." And, as he also said, "They are, perhaps, all the more dangerous on that account."

Even if, for lack of moral and religious imagination in the knower, the idolatrous imagination goes undetected, its effects may be deadly to the soul. For if idolatry absolutizes the relative, then it undermines the solid brickwork of the true norms of our humanity and the divine image within us and puts in its place a foundation of sand and straw. Consider this: What is the real and enduring outcome of imitating Madonna, the Material Girl, and how might that differ from imitating the other Madonna, Mary, Mother of God?

What is more, when the people grow dissatisfied with their idols, they often mercilessly turn on them and consume them with an ungodly wrath. This, it seems to me, is what is happening to the singer and "King of Pop" Michael Jackson. Whether or not he is guilty of pedophilia, the people seem intent upon destroying their fallen idol.

The diabolic imagination

This brings us to the diabolic imagination. In *After Strange Gods,* the Page-Barber Lectures he delivered at the University of Virginia in 1933, T. S. Eliot lamented:

> I am afraid that even if you can entertain the notion of a positive power of evil working through the human agency, you may still have a very inaccurate notion of what Evil is, and will find it difficult to believe that it may operate through men of genius of the most excellent character. I doubt whether what I am going to be saying can convey very much to anyone for whom the doctrine of Original Sin is not a very real or tremendous thing.

In one sense, the diabolic imagination is caused by the disenchantment that follows the self's futile chase after happiness through the idyllic and idolatrous imaginations. Idyllic pursuit of peace, pleasure, or indifference and removal from social responsibility ends in boredom. Likewise, the idol inevitably fails to satisfy the soul. It cannot fill the soul with meaning or joy. There remain only shadows of nothingness: the false pleasures of evil, the last illusions of the Great Deceiver.

In some true sense, the diabolic imagination is latent within each of us, the image of the demonic imprinted by Original Sin on the human soul—what Eliot calls a very "real and tremendous thing." No modern writer has charted the inner workings of the diabolic imagination with such penetrating insight as Dostoevsky. Sometimes Dostoevsky draws dangerously near to giving the diabolic imagination full reign in his characters, as for example in Ivan Karamazov or Stavrogin in *The Possessed.*

Raskolnikov of *Crime and Punishment* is his most sustained observation of the genesis of the diabolic imagination, however. Raskolnikov reaches the height of expression of the diabolic imagination when he says to Sonya in confessing his crime of murder, "I simply killed—killed for myself, for myself alone. . . . I wanted to know, . . . Would I be able to step over, or not! Would I dare to reach down and take, or not."

The diabolic imagination is a terrestrial and cultural descent into the symbolic world of Dante's Inferno. The coordinates that track the fall of the Western self into the diabolic imagination are the loss of the concept of sin and the rise of popular therapeutic justifications and excuses for things that were once thought perverse. Moral norms are redescribed as values relative to self or culture. Human nature is viewed as infinitely malleable and changing. Some go so far as to say it is merely a social construct or fiction. Good and evil are considered matters of perspective.

Persons captivated by the diabolic imagination have outgrown Shakespeare's bawdiness and Hawthorne's irony because they have shed all sense of sin and shame. Presently, the naked thing is viewed as legitimate entertainment, private sport, or recreation. Sex and violence are the flash points of the diabolic imagination, accompanied by unapologetic avarice and egocentricity.

In *After Strange Gods*, Eliot claimed that the "number of people in possession of any criteria for discriminating between good and evil is small. . . . The number of the half-alive hungry for any form of spiritual experience, low or high, good or bad, is considerable." And he concluded: "My generation has not served them very well. Never has the printing press been so busy, and never have such varieties of buncombe and false doctrine come from it. 'Woe unto the foolish prophets, that follow their own spirit and have seen nothing.'" His words ring even truer today than when he first spoke them in the fourth decade of the past century.

Our moral crisis

I have been proposing that we are living within and through a crisis of the moral imagination. Our sense of the drama and struggle over good and evil played out in the human heart and in history has been reduced to the triviality of the afternoon soap opera, to the chase of the action movie, and to the rosy world of the romantic comedy and sitcom, where in the end sentimentality spreads a sweet fragrance most everywhere.

Yes, sentimentality belongs to this diagnosis and description of the crisis of the moral imagination. Sentimentality is the feeble attempt of our lax and liberal culture to claim innocence where there is transgression and perversity, to ignore tragedy in the desperate endeavor to feel comfortable.

Are these the stories of our lives: soap opera, action film, sitcom, and romantic comedy? People go on telling stories because they want to find and clarify meaning for their lives, never just for self-titillation. It matters to every human being that his or her life has meaning and purpose. Yet just as there is right and wrong, there are good stories and bad stories. Stories not only reflect life, they shape it. It is of no small account what stories we tell and what stories we live by.

Plato argued that conversion to that which is moral, that which is just, that which is right and good is like an awakening—like remembering something long forgotten. Symbols, allegories, fables, myths, and good stories have a special capacity to bring back to life the starved or atrophied moral imagination, to bring again to mind what we once knew. Through dramatic depictions of the struggle between good and evil and the presentation of characters that embody and enact the possibilities therein, moral vision clears.

Light comes into our eyes—an illumination of our darkened intellects and a warming of our frozen hearts. Fairy tales are not scientific hypotheses, nor are they practical guides to living. They do something even better, however. They resonate with the deepest qualities of our humanity. They possess the power to draw us into the mystery of morality and virtue. They enable us to envision a world in which there are norms and limits, a world in which freedom respects the moral law or pays an especially high price. Fairy tales show us that there is a difference between what is logically possible and what is morally felicitous, between what is rationally doable and what is morally permissible.

In fairy tales the character of real law belongs to neither natural necessity nor rational determinism. Rather, real law is a comprehensible sign of a primal, unfathomable freedom and of a numinous reality and will. Real law, the realest law, can be obeyed or broken, and in either case for the very same reason—because the creature is both subject of and participant in this primal freedom. Fairy-tale heroes are called to be free and responsible, and thus virtuous and respectful of the moral law.

After a child has read Hans Christian Andersen's *The Snow Queen* or Madeleine L'Engle's *A Wrinkle in Time*, his or her moral imagination is sure to have been stimulated and sharpened. The powerful images of good and evil in these stories show children how to love through the examples of the characters they themselves have come to love and admire. Such memories become the analogues that the moral imagination uses to make real-life decisions, and these memories become constitutive elements of self-identity and character.

A well-fortified and story-enriched moral imagination helps children and adults to move about in the world with moral intent and, ultimately, with faith, hope, and charity. As Flannery O'Connor once said, "Our response to life is different if we have been taught only a definition of faith than if we have trembled with Abraham as he held a knife over Isaac."

5

The Moral Imagination
in an Age of Sentiments

But now all is to be changed.... All the superadded ideas, furnished
from the wardrobe of a moral imagination, which the heart owns
and the understanding ratifies, as necessary to cover the defects of
our naked, shivering nature, and to raise it to dignity in our
estimation, are to be exploded, as a ridiculous, absurd, and antiquated
fashion.

— Edmund Burke, *Reflections on the Revolution in France*

ore than any writer of our time, Russell Kirk
brought to our attention this passage of Burke's on
the moral imagination. From *The Conservative Mind*
(1953) through his posthumously published *Redeeming the Time* (1996), he employed Burke's con-
cept in his social criticism. For Kirk was convinced that only a refurbish-
ment of "the wardrobe of the moral imagination" would dispel the dreari-
ness and moral impoverishment of this utilitarian age. Kirk knew that he
was not alone in this belief, frequently looking to two other modern writers for inspiration, G. K. Chesterton and T. S. Eliot.

In this chapter I want to explore further the meaning of the moral
imagination as it was interpreted by Kirk, Chesterton, and Eliot. This will
not be a genealogy of the idea of the moral imagination, nor in any sense

an exhaustive examination of the pronouncements of these writers on the subject, but rather a congeries of ruminations and reflections inspired by their rich inquiry.

Burke first discusses the *moral imagination* in the sixth edition of *An Enquiry into the Sublime and Beautiful,* published in 1770. To the imagination, he writes, "belongs whatever is called wit, fancy, invention and the like." And when in *An Appeal from the New to the Old Whigs* (1791), he wrote that "Art is man's nature" and that human beings "are as much at least, in a state of Nature in formed manhood as in immature and helpless infancy," the concept of the moral imagination is not far removed from his mind.

Burke understood culture itself as the work principally of the imagination. Imagination synthesizes common experience and works it into image and vision, and this gives birth to art and culture. In "The Pleasures of the Imagination," the eighteenth-century essayist Joseph Addison observed that art is an imitation of nature achieved through this transformative, synthesizing, ordering, and illumining work of the imagination. The imagination, he went on, "has something in it like creation; it bestows a kind of existence. . . .It makes additions to nature." The associationists of the eighteenth century, such as Kames and Blair, credited imagination with the capacity to make metaphors of images and to employ these metaphors to find and suppose moral correspondences in experience. Human culture is different from animal nature precisely because imagination translates the images of sense experience into metaphor and metaphor into art. Thus, accordingly, image and vision are the primary building blocks of civilization.

The book of Proverbs claims that "Where there is no vision, the people perish" (29:18). And Napoleon stated confidently that "Imagination governs the world." Edmund Burke concluded that the French revolutionists were set on a course to deprive a society of its guiding vision. Indeed, they had embraced the work of the Great Depriver himself and were stripping a people of their humanity, robbing them of the historic symbols and images through which morality was pursued and a relationship to a transcendent reality and source of life was discerned. By cutting the lot of humanity off from what Burke called "the unbought grace of life," manners declined, custom was forgotten, public honor diminished, and the gentleness of benevolence was replaced by the ruthless will to power. Ultimately, thought Burke, the French revolutionists were defiling the image of God in man and making a mockery of the dignity of freedom by denying its higher calling. It would not be quite accurate to say that under such conditions human beings become no better than the beasts, for the beasts can manage quite well on the level of uninterpreted sense experience. Rather, when human beings are deprived of "the wardrobe of the moral imagination," their humanity is diminished and becomes twisted, and this is a far more terrifying prospect.

These, then, were Burke's concerns about what lies in store for human beings when the moral imagination is under siege. For while imagination is an innate human capacity, it needs nurture and cultivation. If not properly attended the tea rose withers and thistle grows in its place. If the moral imagination is not fed by religious sentiment and supported by reason it will be replaced by an idolatrous or diabolic imagination. Jacobinism presented a danger of descent into the idolatrous and the diabolical.

These were the dangers that Burke identified in his time; and they are with us today under different historical circumstances. I first read Russell Kirk's *A Program for Conservatives* when I was a senior in high school, and I was impressed even then by his discussion of the moral imagination and its impoverishment. I underlined these passages at that time:

> The modern mind has made utility the basis of politics, and so has left itself defenseless against the self-interest of the fierce egoist and the hard knot of special interests. . . .

> I think that all these crimes and follies are closely bound up with a decay of consciousness of what a reality the unbought

grace of life has been among men, and what a power for their betterment, though it cannot be weighed or tabulated. . . .

The consequences of the neglect or decay of this unbought grace of life being indescribably intricate, any man who begins to examine the problem is oppressed by the dread that his effort will come to no more than a series of sallies into the boundless desolation of modern apathy, without meaning or achievement. . . .To be more specific, then, there are two principle aspects to the degradation of the modern mind. One of these is the effect upon the person; the starving of nearly every man's and woman's higher imagination, so that reason, the faculty which distinguishes the human person in this world from the brutes, is reduced in acuity and in depth; this is the worst thing which can be done to a person, worse than political tyranny or physical injury. And the other aspect is the effect upon the republic, or society: the neglect of those intellectual and moral disciplines which enable us to live together harmoniously, and which are the foundation of free government; this assault upon intelligence, if it is not repelled, must end by subjecting the great majority of men to the mastery of a few managers and manipulators, or else in anarchy.

These observations and admonitions were issued in 1954, and no doubt they reflected Kirk's fresh memory of the New Deal, with its brash pragmatism and the aggressive spirit of political utilitarianism and managerialism that it injected into American life. Through most of the 1970s and '80s there seemed reason to believe, or at least to hope, that at the level of electoral politics the tide was turning away from the New Deal legacy. Yet ironically, political success made conservatives forget the lessons Russell Kirk sought to teach about the priority that must be given to the cultivation and nurture of the moral imagination. Some conservative think tanks deeply inhaled the utilitarian spirit and windily exhaled public policy. Policy study replaced reflective study, as few resources were dedicated to the nurture of the moral imagination through support for literature and the arts.

More might be said about this turn in events. Yet I have promised something else, not a criticism of recent trends in conservative thought and certainly not another lamentation about the decline of the moral imagination. We are seeking to recapture an appreciation of the moral imagination for our lives; and to that end I have two stories to tell. The first is mine. The second belongs to G. K. Chesterton.

In the summer of 1997, my wife June and I hiked in the English Cotswolds, where thatched-roof stone cottages seem to grow right out from the earth and sheep graze on round hillsides spotlighted by the sun between sliding shadows. One morning, I set out on foot and did not cease my wanderings until four in the afternoon. I got lost and found more than once and followed the River Rush toward Bourton-on-the-Water. I thought I spotted Ratty and Mole where the river made a deep bend through a wooded hollow. And off in the distance, just up from the river bank standing on a hill, I spied a stately home that I imagined was Toad Hall.

Nearly a decade before, June and I had visited this part of England. Walking past some small shops along Sheep Street in Stow-on-the-Wold, we came upon a quaint cottage that had a sign out front. It read: Toad Hall. June and I revisited that spot but the sign was gone. We knew that this place had not really been Toad Hall. But I feel sure that I spied the real Toad Hall on my trek through the countryside.

In *Lunacy and Letters*, G. K. Chesterton writes that an "essential mark of the morality of fairyland (a thing [which] is commonly overlooked)" is that "happiness" there, "like happiness anywhere else, involves an object and even a challenge; we can only admire scenery if we want to get past it." Next time June and I visit the Cotswolds, we will look for Toad Hall again. In Kenneth Grahame's story of *The Wind in the Willows*, Toad Hall is a very special place with a profound social significance. Grahame makes Toad Hall a symbol of the social world where friends meet and the imagination flourishes and calls them to service for mutual assistance and shared pleasure. That is why Ratty, Mole, and Badger do not permit their friend to squander away his patrimony, as he does everything else that he owns. And that is why they organize a siege on Toad Hall to take it back from the Weasels and Stouts and other unsavory characters who have illicitly occupied the stately manor during Toad's absence (he has been jailed for stealing and wrecking the notorious red roadster).

The day after my long hike, I spent some time doing the obligatory shopping with my wife. While she arranged for a patchwork coat to be made and sent back home, I walked across the street to a dusty old book shop and found an early edition of G. K. Chesterton's *Autobiography*. The book is not so much an autobiography as it is a series of loosely connected essays in which Chesterton reflects upon what he has learned from life. What he has learned is precisely that the life worth living is the well-imagined life. And the well-imagined life is that in which one discovers first—and only each person can do this for himself, it is not enough to be told that this is so—that the object of one's imagining is to remember what one forgot and that what one forgot is who and what he is and in relation to what and whom he is who he is. In *Orthodoxy*, another semi-autobiographical work and perhaps his best-known book, Chesterton observes:

> Every man has forgot who he is. One may understand the cosmos, but never know the ego; the self is more distant than any star. Thou shalt love the Lord thy God; but thou shalt not know thyself. We are all under the same mental calamity; we have all forgotten our names. We have forgotten what we really are. All that we call common sense and rationality and practicality and positivism only means that for certain dead levels of our life we forget that we have forgotten. All that we

call spirit and art and ecstasy only means that for one awful
instant we remember that we forget.

Now I judge that writing the *Autobiography* and *Orthodoxy* helped
Chesterton himself to awaken to this existential truth. This he accomplished by exercising his memory and imagination. Chesterton hoped to
show others how to do likewise. He begins the *Autobiography* with a recol-
lection of one special childhood memory. And he holds onto that memory
through the whole book. It becomes the book's leitmotif. Thus, imaginatively, Chesterton forges the image of this memory into a symbol that
stands for his personal identity and the goal or *telos* of his life. At the end
of the *Autobiography,* he quotes the phrase that Maurice Baring attributes
to Mary Stuart and which T. S. Eliot later made immortal in the *Four
Quartets:* "In my beginning is my end."

The childhood story that Chesterton recollects is this:

> The very first thing I can ever remember seeing with my own
> eyes was a young man walking across a bridge. He had a curly
> moustache and an attitude of confidence verging on a swagger.
> He carried in his hand a disproportionately large key of shining
> yellow metal and wore a large golden or gilded crown. The
> bridge he was crossing sprang on the one side from the edge
> of a highly perilous mountain chasm, the peaks of the range
> rising fantastically in the distance; and at the other end it joined
> the upper part of the tower of an almost excessively castellated
> castle. In the castle tower there was one window, out of which
> a young lady was looking. I cannot remember in the least what
> she looked like; but I will do battle with anyone who denies
> her superlative good looks.

Chesterton tells us that he viewed this scene from the window and
proscenium of a small theatre that his father erected out of wood and

cardboard, and that the man with the golden key was really just six inches tall. Nevertheless, Chesterton insists, "It is strictly true to say that I saw him [the man with the golden key] before I can remember seeing any-body else; and that so far as memory is concerned, this was the sight on which my eyes first opened in this world. . . . This scene has to me a sort of aboriginal authenticity impossible to describe; something at the back of my thoughts; like the very back-scene of the theatre of things."

This scene with its principal image of the man with the golden key becomes an interpretive symbol of Chesterton's Catholic faith and his own obedience and service to the church. The theatre becomes the stage of the drama of his own life and salvation. He draws the *Autobiography* to a close with this important observation:

> [An] overwhelming conviction that there is one key which can unlock all doors brings back to me my first glimpse of the glorious senses; the sensational experience of sensation. And there starts up again the figure of a man who crosses a bridge and who carries a key; as I saw him when I first looked into fairyland through the window of my father's peepshow. But I know that he who is called Pontifex, the Builder of the Bridge, is called also Claviger, the Bearer of the Key; and that such keys were given him to bind and loose when he was a poor fisher in a far province, beside a small almost secret sea.

Thus, Chesterton dares to suggest that the imagination that came to birth with his childhood play in fairyland became a source and resource of the mature man's belief in God's redemptive role in his life.

In philosophy and literary criticism memory is often associated with the imagination, for memory is thought to provide the images out of which the imagination construes the ultimate shape and meaning that we attach to the world. Imagination is not limited to sensory impressions; nor is life's meaning limited to them. Imagination interprets sensory impressions as it continuously associates them with the images that memory stores and recalls. Imagination even translates these images into metaphors that the self employs to find and suppose moral correspondences in the world. In this way, imagination is a power of perception that sees into the ethical nature of the world through inner connections of agents with their acts.

Chesterton contrasts this suppositional and synthetic character of the imagination with what he calls the science of mental relations. "You cannot *imagine* two and one not making three," he explains. "But you can easily imagine trees not growing fruit." An iron-clad mathematical law is indicated by the first example. In the second case it is supposed on the basis of observation that trees will bear fruit, just as it is supposed, based upon observation and inference, that every man will die a permanent death. But in taking this exercise one step further we can also imagine the possibility that a man might come along who does not die a permanent death but returns to life. One man did just this, and on the basis of his act and the church's memory of it, many succeeding generations of human beings have claimed the same truth for their own lives. This truth is not a postulate of pure reason; but it is an act of the religious imagination.

Christ's resurrection did not abrogate a law of physics, rather it deepened our comprehension of reality and illumined a truth about God in his relationship to the physical universe and his intentions for human beings. For example, St. Paul in his first epistle to the Christians of Corinth defends the resurrection not by claiming a new law of physics, but by *proclaiming* a truth of the imagination held in memory, a hope and confidence so strong that he is willing to stake his mortal life on it. St. Paul was trained in rhetoric and uses unimpeachable logic when he insists, "Now if this is what we proclaim, that Christ was raised from the dead, how can some of you say there is no resurrection of the dead? If there is no resurrection of the dead, then neither has Christ been raised" (1 Cor. 15: 12–13). Just the same, Paul's answer to the question some Corinthians raised about the nature of the resurrected body is, in the last analysis, an achievement of religious imagination. By drawing analogies from nature's processes, he illuminates supernature. Images from nature become metaphors of sacramental significance that reveal and describe transcendent mystery, much as torches in a night garden expose dark, hidden places.

> But you may ask, how are dead people raised? In what kind of body? What stupid questions! The seed you sow does not come to life unless it first has died; and what you sow is not the body that shall be, but a bare grain, of wheat perhaps, or something else; and God gives it the body of his choice, each seed its particular body. (I Cor. 15: 35–38)

In *Lunacy and Letters,* Chesterton ruminates: "I can never understand why it is that those who happen to disbelieve in Christianity do not go back to the great, healthy, permanent human tradition outside Christianity"—the fairy tale. "Because you cannot rise to faith, you need not sink to natural philosophy." Russell Kirk closes his autobiography with a quite similar affirmation about the role that imagination plays in lending purpose to one's life. "Quite conceivably," he concludes in *The Sword of Imagination,* "imagination of the right sort may be so redemptive hereafter as here." This sort of assertion is bound to startle modern people who have learned to think that imagination concerns unreality and that it is not a reliable source of knowledge or truth, that it is not a guide for living.

Burke's wisdom that art is man's nature has been forgotten. Instead, the belief has taken hold that nature is man's nature and culture merely a portion of nature. Burke, Chesterton, and Kirk believe differently. They insist that human imagination is a godlike power. Men may succeed in teaching, or more accurately conditioning, apes to make limited use of human language to communicate. But apes do not come by these powers "naturally." Nor do they "naturally" have the power of imagination necessary to employ this language to compose poetry. They cannot interpret the world with what language they do "learn" from humans. In other words, art is not their nature.

Human nature also entails a purpose that the ape does not experience or know. Burke, Chesterton, and Kirk—Christians and humanists all three—agree that the meaning human beings find in nature depends on faith in a Supreme Being (or God) who endows nature with purpose. They agree that in the act of creating art, men perceive that meaning in nature, as only a creature whom God has created in his very own image can do. In some deep sense, nature, in Western civilization, is a metaphor for Providence, just as the biblical poet of the book of Genesis makes sky a metaphor of the divinity's creative design. This making of metaphor is the work of the moral imagination. When this truth is forgotten or denied, a belief in nature itself cannot be sustained. "Poets, even Pagans," argues Chesterton in his *Autobiography,* "can only directly believe in Nature if they [at least] indirectly believe in God." Modern secularism and atheism are ultimately suicidal for humankind spiritually and morally, a descent into the pit of nihilism. Meaning and purpose, even in philosophical or literary naturalism, is derived from theism, as is, for example, Darwin's belief in evolutionary adaptation and design. Chesterton concludes, "When there is no longer even a vague idea of purposes or presences, then the many-coloured forest really is a rag-bag and all the pageant of the dust only a dustbin."

Chesterton makes an astounding comment in the *Autobiography*—astounding because it expresses a truth obvious yet neglected by most of modern education. He says: "I knew [as a child] that pretending is not deceiving. I could not have defined the distinction if it had been questioned; but that was because it had never occurred to me that it could be questioned. It was merely because a child understands the nature of art, long before he understands the nature of argument." Consider especially the last portion of this statement: "a child understands the nature of art, long before he understands the nature of argument." Here is the strong sense in which images and metaphors are every bit as necessary, if not more so, for human maturation and perfection than the so-called postulates of pure reason or the rational propositions of ethical science. Chesterton continues:

Now it is still not uncommon to say that images are idols and that idols are dolls. I am content to say here that even dolls are not idols, but in the true sense images. The very word images means things necessary to imagination. But not things contrary to reason; no, not even in a child. For imagination is almost the opposite of illusion.

My own experience as a parent and teacher has confirmed the validity of this view of image and imagination. And I believe that we must embrace this truth in raising our children and in cultivating the moral life of every person, whatever his or her chronological age. Indeed, a battle of images is being waged in our culture. Our very *humanitas* is at stake.

In *Decadence and Renewal in the Higher Learning* (1978), Russell Kirk addresses this subject of the image and the age:

When the images of reality have fallen to grossness, why wonder that the notorious Identity Crisis afflicts every corner of society, fastening upon even the more promising natures? Who am I—only a cypher? Do I belong to anything enduring, or signify anything more than a perishable and precarious body? How do I fit into this sensual egalitarian world? Why wonder that some turn to fantastic and perhaps fatal imagery of narcotic, for some the moment's relief from the pain of being human.

And yet it is "the image . . . that can raise us on high, as did Dante's high dream;" or draw "us into the abyss," Kirk continues. "It is [the] matter of the truth or falsity of images" that ought most to concern us in this age, when the written word is being overshadowed by visual imagery that pours in upon us, whether from television, billboards, the movies, video games, or the Internet.

In an essay titled "The Age of Sentiments," collected in *Redeeming the*

Time, Kirk advances his thought on the crisis of moral imagination. He argues that the Age of Discussion, which began in the Enlightenment and characterized modernity, is all but over. We are entering a new era in civilization during which sentiments reign—indeed, we are entering the Age of Sentiments. And this momentous shift in mind and sensibility requires new cultural strategies for the nurture of the moral imagination.

Richard Rorty, the philosopher-trumpeter of postmodernism, argues similarly but with different ends in mind. Rorty observes: "This idea—[a legacy of the Enlightenment]—that reason is 'stronger' than sentiment, that only an insistence on the unconditionality of moral obligation has the power to change human beings for the better, is very persistent." But it is a mistake, Rorty adds. It is the trick of meta-ethical foundationalisms from Plato to Aquinas and Kant, which make us think that there is such a thing as a universal human nature distinguishable from other animal natures by the presence of reason or some spiritual essence. Rorty declares that the situation of our times exposes this lie and illusion as never before. We are being liberated to believe that "nothing relevant to moral choice separates human beings from animals except historically contingent facts of the world, cultural facts."

This is a sleight of hand. Rorty refuses to explore the meaning in the fact that human beings are the *only* creatures to actually create cultures. A Burkean or Kirkian would say that cultural facts and circumstances are not accidents of place and time, but grow out of human nature itself. In other words "art is man's nature" and morality is an inevitable concomitant of that "nature." What constitutes human culture and distinguishes it from the beehive or the wolf pack are images and symbolic articulations that interpret reality, including, inevitably, images of religious and transcendent signification. Human culture is itself the product of the very sorts of ultimate questions raised by countless generations of humanity, questions that Rorty dismisses as meaningless.

Rorty's denial and negation serves the new atheistic pragmatism that he advances. He writes:

The argument does not say: Since there seem to be no gods, there is probably no need to support the priests. It says instead: Since there is apparently no need to support the priests, there probably are no gods. We pragmatists argue from the fact that the human rights culture seems to owe nothing to increased moral knowledge, and everything to hearing sad and sentimental stories, to the conclusion that there is probably no knowledge of the sort Plato envisaged. We go on to argue: Since no useful work seems to be done by insisting on a purportedly ahistorical human nature, there probably is no such nature, or at least nothing in that nature that is relevant to our moral choices.

But however politely Richard Rorty puts the matter—and Rorty is almost always quite polite and nice—the fact is that he is ready to throw out the baby with the bathwater. He correctly notices that there has been a sea change in human culture and civilization that has privileged pragmatism, utilitarianism, and relativism, and so he has decided that there was never anything distinctively "human" about human beings in the first place, nor was there a moral law for human nature. "We are coming to think of ourselves as the protean, self-shaping animal rather than as the rational or cruel animal."

The bathwater certainly is being changed. On this Rorty and Kirk agree. And they agree that the emergent new age is an age ruled by sentiments. But beyond that they part company. Rorty's understanding of sentiment and culture are thin, whereas Kirk's is thick. Rorty is quite content with most any story or image that moves people to get along better with one another. He would like a genial democracy in which feeling good about one another is what is important, and in which "savages" like John in Aldous Huxley's *Brave New World*, whose "neurotic" search for truth and something transcendent disturbs the social concord, would be dealt with therapeutically. Rorty's "decent society" would be Burke's and Kirk's nightmare.

So while both Rorty and Kirk agree that the Age of Discussion is ending and that we are entering the Age of Sentiments, they differ in that Rorty, unlike Kirk, has no regrets about this transition. In Kirk's view, certain norms of human nature and standards of conduct were kept and honored in the Age of Discussion, but with its demise they are in jeopardy of being lost. Kirk is honest about this course of events: the Age of Discussion was not all it was made out to be. If it began with such hardy souls as Addison and Steele, Pope and Dryden, Hume and Smith, and, of course, Edmund Burke, it collapsed into palsied and impoverished Millsian liberalism, Benthamite utilitarianism, and Deweyite pragmatism.

That is why Kirk does not lament its passing too much. He confesses in his essay:

> I suppose I made it clear that I am dragged kicking and screaming into the Age of Sentiments. It is painful enough to be governed by other people's reasoning, without being governed by their sentiments. Yet it should not be thought that I bow down in worship before the late Age of Discussion. For the most part the Age of Discussion was an age of shams and posturing.

Kirk decided to make the best of the situation; even in his later years his optimism about our humanity did not flag. He set out to understand the Age of Sentiments in order to refurbish a moral imagination that might transform and elevate it. Kirk defines sentiment as a human response to the world that lies somewhere between thought and feeling. In other words, it is not synonymous with feeling, as Rorty seems to imply. And it is more than just sensation or emotion. "While it contains too much *feeling* to be merely thought," it does contain thought, and it also "has a large influence over the will." Kirk reminds his readers that for "David Hume and Adam Smith, sentiments exert greater power, and indeed [are] better guides than reason—though Hume remarks in his *Principles of Morals* that sentiment and reason usually coincide." Kirk concludes, "I suppose we may say that for Hume and Smith a sound sentiment is a moving conviction."

That is an important consideration and valuable clue to solving the puzzle presented by our Age of Sentiments. Kirk understands that sentiments and images are quite closely related, and that the quality of the images in a culture helps to determine whether people are moved by sentiment towards a more elevating or a more degrading life.

It is not surprising, in light of all of this, that Kirk is reminded of his philosophical mentor, T. S. Eliot. For Eliot also identified this shift in our civilization from an Age of Discussion to an Age of Sentiments. Eliot understood that in the transition there was great danger as well as the possibility for grace and redemption.

Eliot's phrase and literary invention, the "dissociation of sensibility," captures both the crisis and the potentiality. In his early essay, "The Metaphysical Poets," Eliot proposes that "something . . . happened to the mind of England between the time of Donne or Lord Herbert and the time of Tennyson and Browning. . . . Tennyson and Browning are poets, and they think; but they do not feel their thoughts so immediately as they detect the odor of a rose. Whereas, a thought to Donne was an experience; it modified his sensibility." In the modern poets there occurs a "dissociation of sensibility," such that sensibility is either ungrounded, is mere sentimentality, or it is dissevered from reason.

Eliot concludes that we live in a time when life is shifting from dry thoughts to vaporous sentiments. This is the world of J. Alfred Prufrock and Gerontion. It becomes the mission of the pilgrim persona in *The Wasteland* to begin to put thought and feeling back together. This is a training and discipline of mind and heart. The clues to a world more whole and meaningful are the images, some broken, that lie scattered about in the Wasteland and must be recovered and made sense of through a revivified sensibility and a lively moral imagination. Kirk's own appreciation for the work of Eliot kept him open, therefore, to the possibility that an age of high sentiments might yet "be raised up from the Waste Land. [For] an age moved by high sentiments can be more admirable than an age mired in desiccated discussions."

Russell Kirk fully understood that there is no turning back, that the Age of Sentiments will be with us for some time. But most contemporary conservatives have not read the signs of the times nearly so well as Russell Kirk, G. K. Chesterton, or T. S. Eliot. Much of what we read and hear from conservatives remains stuck in the desiccated Age of Discussion. An obsession with political and economic studies is itself deadening. And, sad to say, by and large conservatives in public life prefer boisterous contest with liberal antagonists in the desolate plain of American politics and the culture wars to the cultivation of the quieter but profoundly more fertile field of the moral imagination. There needs to be a conscious and concentrated turning from the dominant utilitarian spirit to the lessons taught and examples set by geniuses of the moral imagination, whether Virgil, Homer, Dante, Shakespeare, and Dostoevsky, or the more contemporary likes of Faulkner, Flannery O'Connor, Walker Percy, Solzhenitsyn, Anna Akhmatova, and Czezlaw Milosz. They blaze the trail for all of us in our quest for the life well lived.

· *3* ·

Wanderings

in the

Wasteland

6

The Lost Children

The Teachers in the Temple
They did not lift their eyes
For the blazing star of Bethlehem
Or the Wise Men grown wise.
They heeded not a jot and tittle,
They heeded not a jot
The rending voice of Ramah
And the children that were not.

— G. K. Chesterton, "The Neglected Child"

I love them innocently, says God . . .
(That's the way you should love these innocents)
As a father of a family loves the playmates of his son
Who go to school with him.
Innocents for Christ
The children were massacred.

— Charles Péguy, "Innocents"

*I*t would be hard to find two more contrasting books on the theme of children in our culture than John Saward's *The Way of the Lamb: The Spirit of Childhood at the End of the Age* and Henry A. Giroux's *Stealing Innocence: Youth Corporate Power, and the Politics of Culture.*[1] Both Saward and Giroux state that children are at jeopardy—physically, psychologically, and even spiritually. But that is about all they agree on. I suppose it should not be so surprising that two such authors could write on the same topic and differ so radically. After all, we hear chanted the mantra that our children are at grave risk by most everyone these days, those on the Left, those on the Right, and those in between. Saward is a traditional Roman Catholic who is profoundly saddened by the demise of the protection he thinks Christendom once afforded children. "Reverence for the child is the gift of Christianity," he insists, "the gift of Jesus Christ, to the world. It is part of the newness that, according to the Church Fathers, the divine Word incarnate brought into history. And as the world turns away from the Virgin and her Child, who makes all things new, so it falls into the old vice of killing its young." Only a return to a faith that venerates the Virgin Mother and remembers that God became a child for our sakes can put a stop to this violence, says Saward. And he directs us to five modern Christians who each in his or her own special way endeavored to draw out of the great Tradition this vision and value of childhood and apply it to the Christian life as a whole.

Saward juxtaposes and compares the thoughts and lives of St. Thérèse of Lisieux, G. K. Chesterton, Charles Péguy, Georges Bernanos, and Hans Urs von Balthasar to develop and deepen his theology of childhood and his critique of a culture that makes war on children. Saward's eclectic choice of champions of the child and a Christian spirituality of childhood causes conceptual and thematic problems. Some of the comparisons Saward makes seem forced. But overall, he is enormously instructive, for he reveals some marvelous details about the lives and thoughts of these writers.

Henry A. Giroux speaks as a man of the secular and political Left, but he protests no less vehemently than Saward the abuse and exploitation of children in contemporary society. He condemns the commodification of the child by the mandarins of marketing. "Children are increasingly subjected to social and economic forces that exploit them through the dynamics of sexualization, commodification and commercialization," he writes. And Giroux exposes the prevailing prejudice in our culture that favors children of the middle class and demonizes poor and minority youth. He reads the lay of the land from what is an essentially postmodernist perspective and turns to radical economic and educational reform as a means to reclaim the lives of children under a humanistic system of values. Thus, while the first half of *Stealing Innocence* includes chapters on beauty pageants, advertising, drugs, and the corporate takeover of American education, the second half reviews the social and economic philosophies and educational theories of Antonio Gramsci, Paulo Friere, and Stuart Hall, writers whom Giroux recommends as committed to a democratic politics that "addresses the relations of power between youth and adults."

If asked to choose between these two alternatives, I am bound to embrace Saward's Christian spirituality over Giroux's postmodernist liberalism. I say this not without qualification, however. I believe that Saward is basically correct that the war on the child is at bottom a religious matter. Postmodernism rejects, along with other great truths of the Christian faith, the Christian vision of the child as created in the image of God. Yet Saward's presumptions about faith and culture make me a bit nervous. He romanticizes the past and overstates his claims for the singularity and uniqueness of the Christian faith regarding the true value of childhood. I embrace his principal claim that Jesus Christ is the Truth and the Way and that there is no other truth or other way that may be substituted for Him. But Saward's rhetoric causes me unease. For underlying his grim assessment of our culture, with which I also largely agree, there is an element of Christian absolutism and exclusivism that can make one deaf to the truth in others' beliefs. This narrows his audience to exclude not only many non-Christians who may share his concerns, but also many Christians. Perhaps, as an Orthodox Christian who has criticized similar excesses and shortcomings in Orthodox rhetoric, I am overreacting to Saward. But I cannot help thinking that this speech is overly cultic.

This criticism, however, is small potatoes compared to the difficulty I have with Giroux's view of the world—this in spite of the fact that I am in fundamental agreement with his negative diagnosis of advanced capital-ism, his concern about society's neglect of impoverished children, and his outrage at the commodification of the human body by the advertising and entertainment industries. *Stealing Innocence* comprises previously published articles that have been "extensively revised" but even so is not a tightly woven monograph. To lend coherence to the whole, Giroux adds an introductory essay that joins the various themes and issues raised throughout the book. It is to this essay that I will give especially close attention.

At the outset, Giroux states his aim as advancing a view of "cultural politics" that explodes three closely related social myths that combined severely "limit substantive democracy, the welfare of children, and socially engaged scholarship." The first myth is the "end of history." This myth would have us believe that "liberal democracy has achieved its ultimate victory and that the twin ideologies of market and representative democracy now constitute, with few exceptions, the universal values of the new global village." This conflation of democracy with market and corporate power, says Giroux, has caused great harm to children. He spends considerable effort in developing this argument through his discussions of child beauty pageants and the advertising industry's use of children and adolescents as sex objects and stimulants to consumption.

The second myth—inherited, Giroux claims, from the eighteenth and nineteenth centuries—is the myth of the child as innocent. The myth proposes that the innocence of children is rooted in nature itself, and it makes innocence an absolute dogma that transcends "the dictates of history, society, and politics." The dogma is accompanied by a moral imperative: children should be protected and shielded from the corrupted adult world. Giroux argues that this myth actually is harmful to children in two respects. First, while it supplies a reason to protect children, it also denies them "a sense of agency and autonomy." Second, innocence is turned into a tool of bourgeois ideology, which idealizes white middle-class children and demonizes poor and minority children. Thus, according to Giroux, after the shooting at Columbine High School, secular and religious spokespersons used this myth and dogma of innocence to express horror at the killings. On the basis of this myth, such violent behavior was presumed to be abnormal among suburban white middle-class youth. Giroux points out that the same standard is not applied to black youths in the inner cities, who are daily at great risk to become victims of violence. In that demographic, violence is thought to be normal. By definition, young minorities do not share the innocence of their white counterparts, and so when violence takes their lives white politicians and the media do not express Columbine-level outrage. Giroux describes the great attention given to the murder of JonBenet Ramsey as similarly selective and prejudiced.

The last myth that Giroux identifies is the myth of "disinterested scholarship." This myth "embodies the legacy of an ever-expanding commercial culture that harnesses the capacity for public dialogue and dissent to market values." Giroux wants the academy to be more socially engaged and far less beholden to the corporate world that muzzles it with money. He wants the teaching profession to perform the political function of cultural criticism and reform, and he asserts that if teachers taught in such a way the benefit would redound to children, whose lives, bodies, and souls presently are being stolen and consumed by the market and poverty.

Within the academy one frequently encounters Giroux's sort of postmodernist critic. I participated a few years ago in a consultation on religion and children at which one member raised all these issues and attempted to debunk traditional morality and religious views on children as sentimental and romantic. Often, these critics are the most likeable sorts of persons—nice people, one might say. But as I commented to the organizer of the consultation, they are also eerily reminiscent of the liberals who breed nihilistic progeny in Dostoevsky's novels. They are fervent moralists who nevertheless manage to systematically undermine the grounds on which they make their moral protests. I could not agree with Giroux more when he rails against the modern corrupters and exploiters of our children. I applaud when he writes, for example: "Childhood at the

end of the twentieth century is not ending as a historical and social category, it has simply been transformed into a market strategy and a fashion
aesthetic used to expand the consumer-based needs of privileged adults
who live within a market culture that has little concern for ethical considerations, noncommercial spaces, or public responsibilities." But what is
one to make of his blanket claim that "childhood must be understood as a
historical, social, and political construction." I suppose Giroux's answer
would be that this should come as no surprise, since that view of the child
as a social construct is implicit in the passage just cited.

I am attracted to Giroux's ethical concerns about the abuse of children in our culture. But I am also bound to conclude that Giroux has
defined the important subject of his concerns—the child—out of existence. On the terms of his epistemological and anthropological minimalism,
there are no such things as children. There are merely young human beings that are less mature than older human beings. Like their mature counterparts, young human beings live to be autonomous, practice freedom,
and, if fortunate, flourish for a time. For Giroux, traditional religious and
philosophic moral categories such as innocence are nothing more or less
than ideological tools used by the strong to control the weak and by the
rich to subjugate and segregate the poor.

One sees clearly the reductive force of Giroux's positivism on normative ethics when in his chapter about child beauty contests, he pro-
nounces: "As an ethical referent, innocence humanizes children and makes
claims on adults to provide for them with security and protection. But
innocence gains its meaning from a complex set of semiotic, material, and
social registers. . . . Innocence needs to be understood as a *metaphor* [my
emphasis] that is open to diverse uses and whose effects can be both positive and devastating for children." According to Giroux, there is no such
thing as innocence any more than there is any such thing as wickedness.
Both are metaphors. To paraphrase C. S. Lewis, this is indeed the abolition of childhood. Giroux's postmodernist humanism turns out to be at
root profoundly antihuman.

John Saward's principal intuition seems to me correct. Our age's inveterately homicidal character is closely connected with its feticidal, infanticidical, and pedocidal disposition. This disposition constitutes and reflects a crisis of religious belief and moral imagination. Giroux's understanding of reality is so entirely foreign to the biblical and Christian vision of life that there is no imaginable point of mediation. Christians must seek no less than conversion, as they did at the beginning of the faith. Yet Christians themselves seem to have forgotten that the gospel account of Christ's birth does not provide a nice domestic scene but rather a story of a birth threatened by violence. The world has not changed since then, and contemporary Christians cannot afford to be any less vigilant than the magi who confounded Herod, nor can they afford to be less courageous and forthright than was St. Paul at Mars Hill.

Ironically, the sentimentalized and sanitized version of the birth narrative that many if not most contemporary Christians embrace is complicit with contemporary society's rule of silence concerning the violence done to fetuses, infants, and children every day. In this respect, Saward's discussion of Péguy and Chesterton, who insisted on remembering the Holy Innocents, was worth all my reading. These were the children of Bethlehem who bled and died at the hands of Herod and the sword of the state, whose deaths the church commemorates on December 28th in the West and the 29th in the East. Péguy and Chesterton sought to recall in prose and poetry this penitential feast of the church, a feast that has lapsed from the memory of so many Christians. Both issued strong reminders that the redemptive birth of Jesus was hallowed and sanctified by the martyrial blood of infants. Both insisted that the Christian's vision of Mary and her Holy Child in the manger must be accompanied by this memory of the Holy Innocents. Otherwise it was easy to forget that Christ himself was spared that slaughter so that later he might willingly shed his blood for the salvation of all humankind, including all the innocent children whose deaths should never have been. This image of the slaughter of the Holy Innocents makes us look with especial sorrow on such facts as Western abortion, Chinese infanticide, and the deadly impact of AIDS on the children of Africa. There are no equivalent arguments, no principles of ethics or moral rules, that a Christian ethicist like myself can conjure to expose so vividly the compound evil in these deaths of children born and unborn. For by killing our children through abortion or infanticide, by exposing them carelessly to deadly disease and violence, and even by failing to educate them properly, we kill the child within us, that humility and love of life which are God's gifts to us from the child Who is immortal.

7

On the Office of Being a
Good Son or Daughter

I am by no stretch of the imagination a film critic—my expertise is in literature, children's literature in particular. But I have been moved to reflect on a film that was recently aired on one of the cable movie stations, a film I first saw as a young man in 1963. *America, America* captures a crucial theme of children's stories: what it means for a child to assume the moral "office" of being a good son or daughter.

Written, produced, and directed by Elia Kazan, *America, America*'s screenplay is based on the immigrant story of Kazan's own family. The protagonist is a Greek youth named Stavros who grows up in the Anatolian region of Turkey and dreams of going to the United States. In black and white, the film has a documentary quality about it, and Kazan pencils a haunting picture of the hard and oppressed conditions that the Greek and Armenian minority Christian communities endured inside Turkey at the turn of the twentieth century.

Full of youthful bravado and abandon, Stavros resists the injustice of

Ottoman rule and seeks to leave the Old World behind for the New World's promise. Early in the film, Stavros becomes dangerously entangled in the misfortunes of local Armenians who are being rounded up by the Turkish police. Family members drag him home and he is chastised by his mother for putting himself in harm's way. His father leads Stavros into a back room and strikes him hard on the face. After a brief pause, the father then embraces his son, kisses him on both cheeks, and consoles him. The action is startling for its apparent "contradiction." Yet it is a perfectly consistent—even stunning—portrayal of traditional parental love and authority. Punishment is swift and sure, yet lined with strong gestures of affection. The form this love takes and the manner in which such authority is exercised may not please our modern sensibilities, but the contrast with contemporary permissiveness at the very least exposes the latter's weaknesses. There is no tedious negotiation and haggling over who is to blame, who is in charge, or what is the punishment. Justice is swift, love is strong, and patterns of relationship are well defined.

Reconciling responsibility with ambition

Stavros's single-minded pursuit of getting to America may justify seeing him as selfish and inattentive to the needs of his family. In this Middle Eastern culture the obligation of the eldest son to assume responsibility for the well-being of his family is weighty by comparison to our democratized family life. But when his widowed grandmother, who has kept a small treasury hidden in her home, refuses his request for help, Stavros badgers no one. He simply makes up his mind to find another way without assistance from others. The father senses his son's restlessness and imposes a hard task upon him in order to divert Stavros from his goal. He tells Stavros to take all of the family's wealth to Constantinople and see that it is gotten into the hands of an uncle, who will invest it. The investment will enable the entire family to move to the city, where life will be better for all.

Though it will keep him from making his way to America, Stavros accepts the burden of his station as eldest son. But he does not surrender his goal of reaching America—not even after he is tricked, beaten, and robbed of all the family wealth on his long journey to Constantinople. He combines his personal dream with the goal of finding the means to liberate his entire family. His sense of office within the family is the light of that vision and the adhesive that holds his two goals together. Thus, even when he reaches America with nothing but the proverbial shirt on his back, he sends the fifty dollars that an American lady friend gives him to his family as a sign of the earnestness of his love and intentions.

The film chronicles Stavros's struggle to overcome his personal flaws and shortcomings and grow into those habits of character—courage and prudence, trust and perspicacity, patience and perseverance—that he needs to survive and succeed. There is no certainty that Stavros will hold up, that in the end he will not give in to cynicism or become ruthless. The viewer is painfully aware that the whole story has not been told. In *America, America*, Kazan raises the hard questions about growing into manhood and makes it clear that moral character can be either forged or consumed in the heated furnace of the human comedy.

The boy who takes

In the same year that *America, America* was released, *The Giving Tree*, a short illustrated children's book written and drawn by the late Shel Silverstein, was published. In contrast to the poor box-office reception of *America, America*, *The Giving Tree* was an immediate success and has remained a best-selling children's book ever since. Like *America, America*, it invites reflection on the meaning of being a son.

With few words and minimalist line drawings, *The Giving Tree* tells the story of the relationship of a boy and a tree, who like a mother gives the whole of herself to the son. The boy asks for and takes all that the tree can give: her leaves, her fruit, her limbs, and her trunk. Virtually every demand he makes of the tree is to satisfy his personal appetites. The boy grows into adulthood, but the reader is not sure whether he ever marries or has children. He says to the tree that he wants a family and announces his need for a house. He asks the tree if she can give him one. The tree replies that she has no house, but offers him her branches so that he will be happy. But the boy never again mentions a family. When the boy returns, he is miserable and wishes he had a boat to take him far away. He asks the tree if she has a boat, and she replies by offering to let him cut down her trunk to make one. For long periods of time, the boy neglects to visit the tree, which, Silverstein writes, makes the tree sad. At the end of the story, the boy returns to the tree after a long absence. He is a tired, crooked, lonely old man. Nevertheless, the tree welcomes the boy back despite his neglect and offers him all that she has left: a stump on which to sit and rest.

If the tree, and not the boy, is the principal subject of Silverstein's book, then a generous reading would interpret the tree as a model of unqualified parental love. If the boy is the principal subject then I cannot think of much to commend in his behavior—or in the book. At best he may serve as a negative example of selfishness that exceeds the limits of the legitimate need for love that quite naturally attends childhood.

Several years ago a symposium on *The Giving Tree* was published in the monthly magazine *First Things*. In the discussion, one of the distinguished participants, Professor Jean Bethke Elshtain of the University of Chicago, recalled the angry response of her adult daughter to the book. When Elshtain first gave the book to her, she received it enthusiastically: "Shel Silverstein. He's pretty famous, isn't he?" But after reading *The Giving Tree* she called it "a vicious book." She said, "I'm surprised. I thought he was supposed to be a good children's author." When Elshtain asked her daughter to explain what her objections were, she responded:

Well, just look at the tree. It has nothing left [at the end of the story]. It's just a stump. And the boy, or man, is just constantly "gimme gimme" and he expects the tree to give him anything he wants or needs. He never really grows up. He's just spoiled. He's like so many Americans. He thinks there should always be someone to satisfy his wants any time he wants anything.

The filial office

I recognize that *America, America* and *The Giving Tree* belong to two vastly different genres and that a host of objections could be raised to any comparisons one might venture about them. Nevertheless, a comparison of the two is illuminating: it invites reflection on the moral meaning of the parent-child relationship and in particular calls attention to what I have called the office of being a good son or daughter.

The Giving Tree leaves the strong impression that human beings are from the start autonomous agents who act principally on their own behalf and choose when to relate to others on the basis of appetite and impulse. Feelings and emotions are what are principally at stake. The tree is happy when the boy comes to visit and sad when he leaves. The boy has desires that when satisfied by the tree make him happy, at least for a time. *America, America*, on the other hand, insists that being a child means being the child of particular parents and a member of a family. We do not choose this status. It is a given. We come into the world related to others. Feelings and emotions are in the mix but we become fully human only when we embrace duties and obligations the purpose of which is to secure the well-being of everyone concerned. Character—not happiness—is the measure of our success.

God has made children so that they naturally enjoy playing roles and want to be good sons or daughters. And children naturally look forward to becoming good parents themselves one day. Our modern notion of autonomy not only lacks moral seriousness, it demeans childhood by depicting it, with its dependency, as something that needs to be overcome in order to become free and independent. An older and more profound wisdom says that dependency is not a defect to be overcome, but is rather a characteristic of the human condition. Rather than take from others only in order that we might need them no longer, we must build upon this "natural" dependency of children and transform it into the foundation for a moral sense of human responsibility and duty. Developing a better understanding of the filial office may aid us in undoing our impoverished understanding of human freedom, which is divorced from the increasingly forgotten riches of family and community.

The Latin roots of "office" lend to it the connotations of sacrifice and duty. It is a word that cuts deeply against the grain of our culture's individualism and understanding of freedom as nothing more than personal autonomy. When applied to parenthood or childhood it entails profound moral content and purpose, for it grounds goodness and character solidly in a public and even political world. This grounding saves goodness from becoming a mere philosophical abstraction or from being reduced to modern psychological notions of self-fulfillment. It reminds us that goodness is "no good" unless it obtains a "form" and "body" along with an abiding purpose the horizon of which transcends the self. Goodness is not some "thing" that the individual possesses. It is, rather, the product of virtuous behavior that binds human community. For children, this community is principally the family. By conscientiously embracing the responsibilities of the "office" of being a son or daughter, a child is rendered truly human.

The Good Son

No children's story in all of Western literature more powerfully impresses upon its reader what I have been saying about the "office" of being a good child than does Carlo Collodi's *Pinocchio*. When I teach *Pinocchio* in the college classroom, some students quickly observe that Pinocchio lacks a strong parental figure, that in practical terms he is an orphan. But other students challenge this interpretation, pointing out that although Pinocchio and Geppetto are separated through most of the story, the carpenter who has made the puppet is an important parent figure. Still other students observe that the blue-haired fairy is both a sister and a mother to Pinocchio. She challenges the puppet to act responsibly throughout the story by assuming a variety of human and animal identities to protect, guide, and discipline the impetuous puppet.

Those who have seen only the Disney movie version of *Pinocchio* or read abridged picture-book tellings of the story typically think of Pinocchio as a wooden puppet that is transformed into a real, flesh-and-blood boy. And, certainly, it is on that note that the original tale ends. Nevertheless, Collodi works hard to depict Pinocchio's path to real boyhood as a struggle to be not just human but specifically a good *son*. Indeed, Pinocchio's desire to be a genuine flesh-and-blood boy depends utterly on how well he succeeds in behaving as a son toward Geppetto and the blue-haired fairy. In other words, the virtues and habits of character that Pinocchio obtains through his many trials and tribulations gain him a "body" and purpose in filial identity and responsibility. This office of sonship is the invisible human body that Pinocchio wears even before he is transformed into a being of human flesh.

Disney's movie ends just after Pinocchio saves Geppetto from the belly of the great whale (a shark in the original) and leaves out important events that follow in Carlo Collodi's story. For in that story, Pinocchio labors unselfishly to support his aged father, who is no longer able to care for the two of them. And when the puppet hears that the blue-haired fairy has fallen ill and is in the hospital, he gives over the small sum that he has saved to buy himself a new suit for her care. Collodi leaves no room for doubt: It is in return for his love of and respect for his parents that Pinocchio's wish to be a *real* boy is fulfilled. In a dream, the blue-haired fairy announces to him:

> Brave Pinocchio! In return for your good heart, I forgive you all your past misdeeds. Children who love their parents, and help them when they are sick and poor, are worthy of praise and love, even if they are not models of obedience and good behavior. Be good in the future, and you will be happy.

Is this not a far more satisfying account of happiness than the one that *The Giving Tree* gives? Does it not ring more true?

"I've got no strings . . ."

The lure and great power of *Pinocchio* resides in the truth it conveys through its central metaphor of the wooden puppet. In some real way, we all are born puppets who grow into flesh-and-blood human beings: we all start out dependent and mature into persons able to exercise our freedom responsibly. There are many stumbles and spills along the way, but we, like Pinocchio, eventually claim our actions as our own. We do not arrive in this world with a fully formed moral character in the same way that we bear certain traits of personality or an emotional disposition. Moral character is built upon the stuff of heredity and environment and the particular circumstances of our lives.

Yet the self that is a moral actor who exercises freedom and choice is much more than the sum of these factors. The virtues constitute character, and yet even they cannot be taught and learned the way mathematical logarithms are learned. The virtues are not so simply obtained as by attending a course in business ethics or memorizing the Ten Commandments. Virtues are habits formed by doing, and in order to grow in strength they require exercise in responsible relation to others and in social offices and institutions. Today, we desperately need stories like *Pinocchio* and *America, America* to help us to recover these truths for our lives and for our children in a culture that not only seems to have forgotten them, but seeks continuously to replace them with new and dangerous dogmas.

8

Family and Christian Virtue in a Post-Christian World:
The Vision of John Chrysostom

O f the many quotable passages from the writings of St. John Chrysostom, the most often cited is located in his twentieth homily on Ephesians: "If we regulate our households [properly] . . . we will also be fit to oversee the Church, for indeed the household is a little Church. Therefore, it is possible for us to surpass all others in virtue by becoming good husbands and wives."[1] Frequently, this passage has been cited as a text supporting high sacramental interpretations of marriage. Rarely has there occurred sustained discussion of what might best be described as Chrysostom's ecclesial vision of the Christian family and household. That is my task here. I also want to show how this vision enables Christians to understand better what truly is at stake for the church in the contemporary debate about the family and its role in moral upbringing.

Chrysostom lived at a moment of genuine cultural crisis. The pagan culture of antiquity was in decline, and Christianity had become a social force with which to be reckoned. It was not yet clear, however, what shape a future Christian culture might take. Chrysostom was one of a minority of Christian apologists (St. Basil was another) who voiced serious misgivings about the emerging Christian order. Like Basil, he brought the spirit of monastic reform into his critique of society. He inveighed against the moral laxity of self-professed Christians and their excessive preoccupation with material possession, power, and social status. This reform spirit drove Chrysostom's ecclesiology as he struggled to steer a course that would lead neither to an imperial church nor to a cake-frosting version of Christianity for the masses. His example is relevant all over again for churches today as they enter a definitively post-Christendom era marked by cultural deterioration and are faced with difficult choices about how to relate to the emerging hegemonic secularity.

Chrysostom might easily have succumbed to the temptation to promote the moral rehabilitation of the family as a means of securing societal stability. We hear repeatedly today from religious sources—Protestants, Roman Catholics, and Orthodox alike—that the family is of social value as a bulwark against social decay. Recent presidential campaigns have made the family an issue as we have heard from candidates how important strong and healthy families are to the American way of life. Less clear in the political rhetoric is what these family values actually amount to or in what they are grounded.

Chrysostom did not ignore the sociological dimension or function of the family. On one occasion he said, "When harmony prevails [in the household], the children are raised well, the household is kept in order, and neighbors, friends, and relatives praise the result. Great benefits, both for families and states, are thus produced."[2] He, however, subordinated this societal function of the family to its ecclesial role. Christian marriage and family are a vocation in the church to build up the kingdom of God. In order to fulfill this vocation, the Christian family must practice a spiritual and moral discipline that resists the ways of the world. Chrysostom was clear about the proper source of family morality: the life of Christ and the commandments.

Chrysostom's vision of the ecclesial family was radical when he preached it in the fourth century, and it is equally radical in our secular culture. Living after Christendom, we as spouses and parents can no longer assume that our children will be nurtured in biblical and Christian norms outside of the church, because these standards of behavior and moral norms no longer govern in our culture. It should be obvious to Christian spouses and parents how truly radical their vocation as family is within contemporary society; we seem regrettably prone to forget what actually is entailed in being married "in the Lord." The printed and electronic media bombard us with powerful and seductive alternatives to the demanding, disciplined life to which the Christian family is called biblically and through the marital rites of the church. It is easy to think of the Christian family as merely a church-going version of any number of comfortable and idealized sitcom families or, alternatively, to despair of traditional marriages and families altogether.

Chrysostom addresses us when he urges the churches to make strenuous and sustained efforts to cultivate and restore the vision of the family as an ecclesial entity and a mission of the kingdom of God. Sociologists tell us that for vast numbers of Americans, the family has lost its public meaning and outlook. It is being redefined as a haven of private living, consumption, and recreation. Civic-mindedness has been replaced with hunger for privacy. Personal sacrifice for children and community has been replaced by self-centeredness and hedonism. Chrysostom's ecclesial vision of the family speaks to this disintegration of community, but it does so in a fashion that can only look strange even to people who otherwise worry about the privatization and moral privation of the family. While sociologists and politicians contend that the family is in trouble because it is not contributing as it should to the formation of viable community and civic virtue, Chrysostom argues that the Christian family is a calling to community in service to God and his kingdom that spreads into the whole of society.

Chrysostom's teachings on marriage and family push us into a much larger debate that is at the center of contemporary Christian ethics—a debate over the prospects for the Christian faith and morality generally within our secular order. As I have suggested, there are those who cling to the empty hope that some version of Christendon is still possible and, hence, that Christian ethics can still be done in old and familiar ways of correlating Christian truth with norms and institutions found within the culture. Others pin their hope on a more modest goal of designing a new public theology for a pluralistic order. Efforts in this direction go on in diverse and even opposing ideological camps, among neo-conservatives, mainline Protestants, and liberal as well as neo-Thomist Catholics. Still others are persuaded that Christendom has ended and that it never was a good idea in any case. Many of these people have turned to alternative models of a confessing church, whose "main political task" lies "not in the personal transformation of individual hearts or the modification of society," but rather, as Stanley Hauerwas and William H. Willimon have put it, "in the congregation's determination to worship Christ in all things . . . and to build up an alternative polis"—that being the church.[3] The contending parties fling accusations back and forth at one another about whether their respective proposals for the church are too accommodating towards the culture or too sectarian.

Chrysostom helps us to see that this perennial question about the appropriate relationship of the church to the culture is reflected in microcosm within the Christian family. With respect to the contemporary debate. I want to demonstrate how Chrysostom's way of stating the relation of family to church and church to culture eludes some of the facile categories in which we have learned to pigeonhole other points of view. Chrysostom was neither sectarian, accommodationist, nor triumphalist. He resisted the Eusebian-Christian imperialism of his day. He was not taken with the Constantinian-Theodosian theocratic synthesis of church and state that, as later codified by Justinian, provided the ideological framework for Byzantine theocracy. Nor did he propose that the church retreat into the catacombs or hold the opinion that the only pure and true Christianity was restricted to the monastery. Rather, Chrysostom's idea of an evangelical and socially responsible Christian faith was bound up with the pastoral and moral theology he addressed to Christian parishioners and Christian rulers alike. In all that he said about the nature of the church-world relationship, Chrysostom returned again and again to the belief of the church fathers that salvation is accomplished from within the church through its process of making the kingdom of God present to an unbelieving world. And he viewed the family as an ecclesial entity that figured centrally in this salvific process.

The "ecclesial" household

As Gerhardt B. Ladner has observed, by the end of the fourth century, especially in the East, "the ascetic and mystic and the ruler shared between them as it were true kingship. Reformed in the royal image of God, they represented two different but equally high orders of mankind."[4] The Constantinian-Theodosian initiatives to establish a Christian commonwealth, formalized by the Emperor Justinian in the sixth century, tipped the balance away from the ascetic and mystic toward the ruler. The emperors increasingly asserted a "quasi-sacerdotal position [for themselves] in the Church, and generally made it understood that the value of all acts of reform in the Church and empire flowed directly from the fact that they were put into effect by, or on the command of, the emperor."[5]

Early in his career Chrysostom resisted these trends toward imperial domination of the church and society. He did so by championing monastic claims of true "kingship" over the Eusebian conception of the king-philosopher. This is a clear aim of his short treatise, "A Comparison Between a King and a Monk" (ca. 380). As Ladner puts it: "There was one great exception to the eastern development of [the] Basileia ideology: the thought and life of St. John Chrysostom."[6] The truly significant turn in Chrysostom's thought came, however, as he struggled with his pastoral and homiletic duties at Antioch and later in Constantinople. In these settings, Chrysostom became convinced "that, apart from the privilege of marriage, the Christian who lived in the world had the same obligations as the monk."[7] While expounding a churchly interpretation of the Christian household as a mission of the kingdom of God in the world, he also anticipated and answered the later Byzantine alternatives of (1) envisioning the church as the sacramental organism that whispers in the emperor's ear and sacralizes an imperial order, and (2) endorsing the view that the monks are the only true representatives of holiness in a compromised and sinful world.

At the close of his Antiochene ministry, Chrysostom wrote the "Address on Vainglory and the Right Way for Parents to Bring Up Their Children" (ca. 386–387). There he spoke "of a child's soul as of a city in which the King of the universe intends to dwell, and God's earthly representative in this city is not the emperor, but the child's father." "Nothing," concludes Ladner, "could be less 'Eusebian' than this conception of the Kingdom of God on earth, and it is not surprising that John Chrysostom perished as a martyr for Christian ethical principles in resistance"[8] to the emerging and solidifying ideology of a Christian empire.

From this point on, Chrysostom sought to "reform the 'Polis' within the 'Basileia'."[9] He increasingly identified the proleptic presence of the kingdom of God not primarily with the empire or the cloistered monastery but with the near and familiar Christian household. The cardinal "marks" of the kingdom, Chrysostom insisted, are compassion, love of neighbor, and hospitality toward friends and strangers alike. The Christian household, he maintained, is an exact image of the *ecclesia* when it puts into practice the gospel teaching about our behavior toward one another and toward God.[10]

Chrysostom thought of the Abrahamic household as the ancient biblical type of the Christian "ecclesial" household. He maintained that the Abrahamic household kept and practiced in an exemplary fashion those virtues of the kingdom of God that should belong to the people of God in

106

order that they may receive the Messiah when he comes. In his homily on Acts 20:32, Chrysostom says:

> Make yourself a guest-chamber in your own house; set up a bed there, set up a table there and a candlestick. For is it not absurd, that whereas, if soldiers should come, you have rooms set apart for them, and show much care for them, and furnish them with everything, because they keep off from you the visible war of this world, yet strangers have no place where they may abide? Gain a victory over [prevail over] the Church. . . . Surpass us in liberality: have a room to which Christ may come; say, "This is Christ's cell; this building is set apart for Him. . . . Abraham received the strangers in the place where he abode himself; his wife stood in the place of a servant, the guests in the place of masters. He knew not that he was receiving Christ; knew not that he was receiving Angels; so that had he known it, he would have lavished his whole substance. But we, who know that we receive Christ, show not even so much zeal as he did who thought that he was receiving men. . . . Let our house be Christ's general receptacle."[11]

Clearly Chrysostom has in mind something even more concrete than the actual network of human family or household relations. The physical dwelling itself is realized as "Christ's general receptacle." Abraham's tent is the Old Testament type of the Christian dwelling, which has become the house of God. When the members of the household provide for guests and greet them in their home, the dwelling itself serves as the body of the Lord.

Elsewhere in his homilies on the Book of Acts, Chrysostom filled this metaphor of the house of God with its members and their relations. "Let the house be a Church, consisting of men and women. . . . 'For where two,'

He saith, 'are gathered together in My Name, there am I in the midst of them.'"[12] Hospitality was such an important virtue for Chrysostom that he held that it should figure in the selection of one's spouse. Abraham sent his servant to his own country to find a wife for his son Isaac, and the servant determined through prayer that he should choose the woman who offered him water not only for himself but also for his camels (Gen. 24:11–14). The servant was sent looking for such a bride for Isaac, writes Chrysostom, because "everything good" that happened to the household "came because of hospitality. . . . Let us not see only the fact that he asked for water, but let us consider that it shows a truly generous soul not only to give what is asked but to provide more than is requested."[13] This sort of cultivation of a righteous household, he concludes, is a means of seeking and receiving the kingdom of heaven. "'Thou who receivedst Me,' He saith, 'into thy lodging, I will receive thee into the Kingdom of My Father; thou tookest away My hunger, I take away thy sins; thou sawest Me a stranger, I make thee a citizen of heaven; thou gavest Me bread, I give thee an entire Kingdom, that thou mayest inherit and possess.'"[14]

Chrysostom cites the home of Aquila and Priscilla as a quintessential New Testament example of an "ecclesial" household. These two workers in the Lord unselfishly opened their home to St. Paul and other disciples of Christ. "It was no small excellency, that they had made their very house a Church. . . ." And Paul exhorted the Corinthian Christians to greet one another "with the holy kiss . . . as a means of union: for this unites, and produces one body."[15] As Gus Christo has summarized, Chrysostom held that "a Christian home's transformation into the Church . . . or a church, happens when its occupants salute each other with the holy kiss . . . are hospitable to people and remain free of deceit and hypocrisy."[16] Such a home or church becomes a site from which Christ draws the rest of the public world into his kingdom. This in turn is described as a liturgical and sacramental action. "Charity," Chrysostom once exclaimed, is "a sacrament. . . . For our sacraments are above all God's charity and love."[17]

The Christian family as mission of the kingdom of God

In order to emphasize the larger ordained purposes and calling of the Christian family, Chrysostom repeatedly returned to the stories of the Abrahamic household, even Abraham's willingness to follow God's command and offer his only son in sacrifice. Yet the Old Testament story of Hannah and her son Samuel is the one he most often invoked to illumine the unselfish and heroic qualities required by God of those who assume the office of parenthood. Chrysostom's use of the story shifted over the years, however, from an early defense of monasticism to a later focus on the responsibility of Christian parents to attend consciously to raising their children as true Christians, and not just nominal ones.

In his early work, *Against the Opponents of the Monastic Life,* Chrysostom called on parents to raise their children unselfishly to be fit inheritors of the kingdom of heaven. This entailed especially, though not exclusively, preparing them for the monastic life. Chrysostom described Hannah as an exemplar of such responsible and unselfish parenthood. She "gave birth to one child and did not expect to have another. Indeed, she had scarcely given birth to him, and this after many tears, for she was sterile.... When he no longer needed to be nursed, she immediately took him and offered him up to God, and she ordered him to return to his father's house no longer, but to live continually in the temple of God."[18] Thus it was that Hannah fulfilled the community's office of a parent, by dedicating her son to God and to the well-being of his people. For "when God had turned away from the race of the Hebrews because of their profuse wickedness ... [Samuel] won back God's favor through his virtue and persuaded him to supply what had been given previously.... Such," concludes Chrysostom, "is always the reward for giving our possessions to God ... not only possessions and things, but our children."[19]

More than a decade after he wrote these words, during his ministry in Antioch, or perhaps even later during his episcopacy at Constantinople, Chrysostom returned to the very same story in his homily on Ephesians

6:1–3. In the context of instructing parents on how to raise their children, he grants that it is not necessary to raise them as monks; it is enough that they be raised as good Christians.[20] Still, of "the holy men and women of old," he cites Hannah as the example to imitate. "Look at what she did. She brought Samuel, her only son, to the temple, when he was only an infant!"[21] Chrysostom uses the story to emphasize the importance of raising children on Scripture. "Don't say, 'Bible reading is for monks; am I turning my child into a monk?' . . . It is necessary for everyone to know Scriptural teachings, and this is especially true for children."[22]

This instruction that parents should raise their children not to become monks but just to be good Christians is not at all inconsistent with Chrysostom's earlier use of the Hannah and Samuel story in *Against the Opponents of the Monastic Life*. The cardinal obligation and task of Christian parenthood remains the same: to prepare the child for service to God and his people. Hannah "gave Samuel to God, and with God she left him, and thus her marriage was blessed more than ever, because her first concern was for spiritual things."[23]

In an ancient prayer of the Armenian rite of matrimony, the priest beseeches God to plant the couple "as a fruitful olive tree, in the House of God, so that living in righteousness, in purity, and in godliness, according to the pleasure of Thy beneficent will, they may see the children of their children and they may be a people unto Thee."[24] This liturgical prayer emphasizes the ecclesial nature of Christian marriage and family. This is to seek the kingdom of God. To raise children in virtue and righteousness renders them "a people unto" God. In *Against the Opponents of the Monastic Life*, Chrysostom quotes 1 Timothy 2:15: "'They will be saved through bearing children, if they remain in faith and love and holiness, with modesty.'"[25] Hannah's "wisdom" was a matter of comprehending through faith that by dedicating to God "the first-fruits of her womb" she might "obtain many more children in return."[26] Her attention to spiritual things was not a retreat into the private self or family; it was an affirmation of the existence of a community of faith to which she belonged and in which she held the divinely commissioned office of parent. God in turn bestowed upon her the growing company of that community.

Ephesians 5 and the ecclesial marriage

John Chrysostom's strongest statements about the ecclesial calling of Christian husbands and wives, fathers and mothers, comes, not surprisingly, in his homily on Ephesians 5:22–23: "Wives, be subject to your husbands, as to the Lord. For the husband is the head of the wife just as Christ is the head of the church, the body of which he is the Savior." Feminist theologians have regarded this passage as a central piece of what they characterize as the theologization of antiquity's structures of domination.[27] Other theologians have maintained that there is more Christianizing of the marital relationship than the critics admit in this and other *Haustafeln* passages. John Howard Yoder, for example, argues that submission here assumes the character of a revolutionary subordination through the Pauline theology of *agape* and freedom in Christ.[28]

Virtually all who write on this passage, however, agree that it reflects the Pauline author's strong interest in ecclesiology. As Elisabeth Schüssler Fiorenza conjectures at one point in her analysis of Ephesians 5, "The reason for . . . [its] theological shortcomings might be the author's interest in clarifying the relationship between Christ and the Church, whose unity is his primary concern in the rest of the letter."[29] Chrysostom's interpretation of this passage is strongly ecclesiological. He believes that it establishes a sacramental and even ontological relationship between the institution of marriage and the church. God's economy is channeled first of all through the Body of Christ, the church; the peace of the world is guaranteed by the peace of that Body. And the peace of the church is a discipline and task of the Christian family; and the peace of the church is strengthened by the harmony and good order of a godly household. Thus, reasons Chrysostom, the wife does not obey the husband ultimately for "her husband's sake," but "primarily for the Lord's sake."[30] Just as the husband loves his wife "not so much for her own sake, but for Christ's sake."[31]

After discussing the proper attitude of the wife toward her husband, Chrysostom considers the proper attitude of the husband toward his wife. Keeping in mind St. Paul's analogy of the husband as the head of the wife, Chrysostom works together Christic and ecclesial metaphors, exhorting each husband to

> be responsible for the same providential care of... [your wife], as Christ is for the Church. And even if it becomes necessary for you to give your life for her, yes, and even to endure and undergo suffering of any kind, do not refuse. Even though you undergo all this, you will never have done anything equal to what Christ has done. You are sacrificing yourself for someone to whom you are already joined, but He offered Himself up for one who turned her back on Him and hated Him.[32]

Both husband and wife must imitate the Lord, but the greater burden is on the husband, precisely because he is in the position of greater power. He who would view himself as master is called upon to be servant in the likeness of Christ, who is the head of the church. "What sort of satisfaction could a husband himself have, if he lives with his wife as if she were a slave, and not a woman of her own free will," asks Chrysostom. "Suffer anything for her sake, but never disgrace her, for Christ never did this with the Church."[33] In his condescending and sacrificial relationship to the church, Christ becomes the example husbands must follow in their relationship to their wives: "Imitate the Bridegroom of the Church."[34] Christ condescended to take the church as his bride even though "the Church was not pure. She had blemishes, she was ugly and cheap. Whatever kind of wife you marry, you will never take a bride like Christ did ... you will never marry any one estranged from you as the Church was from Christ. Despite all this, he did not abhor or hate her for her extraordinary corruption."[35] Rather, Christ loved the church, in order that she might be sanctified (Eph. 5:25–27). The ecclesial metaphor reigns throughout Chrysostom's strong advice about spousal attitudes and conduct within the marital relationship. The nature of the church and the nature of marriage illumine each other.

In this theology, the Christian family figures as the primal and sacramental human community in which kenotic and agapeic love are learned and rehearsed. Husband and wife share this love within the conjugal relationship, and in turn, they communicate this love to the children through their parental care. Furthermore, the Christian family, rehearsed in and equipped with the right virtues, is an arena of ascetic combat with the demons of personal and public life. This *askesis,* this struggle, not only perfects persons but also deepens community.

The virtues of the Christian family

Chrysostom admired the historic virtues of classical culture. Yet he was not to be counted in the company of those Christian writers who thought that the classical and Christian virtues were identical, always complementary, or easily correlated with one another. When Chrysostom looked out at the culture, he saw that Christians were captives to its human-centered standards of success and happiness, and he pleaded with Christian parents to foster another kind of character in their children.

> If a child learns a trade, or is highly educated for a lucrative profession, all this is nothing compared to the art of detachment from riches; if you want to make your child rich, teach him this. He is truly rich who does not desire great possessions, or surrounds himself with wealth, but who requires nothing. . . . Don't worry about giving him an

influential reputation for worldly wisdom, but ponder deeply how you can teach him to think lightly of this life's passing glories; thus he will become truly renowned and glorious.... Don't strive to make him a clever orator, but teach him to love true wisdom. He will not suffer if he lacks clever words, but if he lacks wisdom, all the rhetoric in the world can't help him. A pattern of life is what is needed, not empty speeches; character, not cleverness; deeds, not words. These things secure the Kingdom and bestow God's blessings.[36]

Stoic influences alone cannot account for this passage. The Beatitudes, which Chrysostom described as the very constitution of the kingdom of God, lie very near to its surface, together with a biblically founded eschatological hope.

The Bible, said Chrysostom, is the basic primer and lesson book for the virtues of the kingdom that God charges parents to teach their children. Scripture provides the narratives of the lives of patriarchs and matriarchs, parents and siblings, who struggled in God's presence to maintain a way of life distinct though not necessarily separate from the world. In *Address on Vainglory and the Right Way for Parents to Bring Up Their Children,* Chrysostom pioneered what might be regarded as one of the first Christian curriculums for children's Bible study. The responsibility for such education, however, resides first with the parents. Chrysostom commended especially the stories of Cain and Abel, Jacob and Esau, Joseph and his brothers, Hannah and Samuel, and the like. His method is worth observing.

Much of Chrysostom's discussion is concerned with identifying biblical models for relations between parents and children and of siblings with each other. For example, he encourages parents to juxtapose the stories of Cain and Abel and of Jacob and Esau in the manner of a diptych, drawing out the distinct lessons of each story as well as the common themes within both narratives of sibling rivalry, envy, and fratricide. He urges parents to tell the stories of Cain and Abel and Jacob and Esau, not once, but repeatedly. Then they should say to the child:

> "Tell me the story of those two brothers." And if he begins to relate the story of Cain and Abel, stop him and say: "It is not that one that I want, but the one of the other two brothers, in which the father gave his blessing." Give him hints but do not as yet tell him their names. When he has told you all, spin the sequel of the yarn, and say: "Heed what occurred afterwards. Once again the elder brother, like in the former story, was minded to slay his brother...."[37]

In his twenty-first homily on Ephesians, Chrysostom gave his rationale for this instruction and pleaded its importance for Christian living.

> Don't think that only monks need to learn the Bible; children about to go into the world stand in greater need of Scriptural knowledge. A man who never travels by sea doesn't need to know how to equip a ship, or where to find a pilot or a crew, but a sailor has to know all these things. The same applies to the monk and the man of this world. The monk lives an untroubled life in a calm harbor, removed from every storm, while the worldly man is always sailing the ocean, battling innumerable tempests.[38]

From the perspective of Chrysostom's vision of Christian family and virtue, strategies for the revitalization of the family and preservation of society based on the Constantinian model are theologically misdirected. Once one defines Christian existence and tradition in merely sociological terms, a certain kind of ecclesiology and definition of the Christian family emerges. The family is a training ground for virtues that first have to do with the well-functioning of the secular polity—a worthy enough goal, but not what lies at the heart of the vocation of Christian parenthood and family. Nor in these post-Christendom times is it helpful to seek to counteract the privatism in the American family with social ministry, as liberal Protestants and liberal Roman Catholics seem to think.[39] The Christian family, weakened and secularized by powerful cultural forces of privatism, narcissism, and consumerism, is scarcely the agent of social change in any case.

There is a necessary interim step missing in such calls to commit the Christian family to social transformation. The Christian family can receive a public vocation only after it has first engaged in the struggle for the kingdom of God. The jargon of the Christian activists: "intimacy," "shared decision making," "peacemaking," "cooperative projects," and the like, is hardly distinctive; nor is it in advance of the other kinds of progressivism in the culture that fail to provide a transcendent imperative for ethical behavior. Chrysostom insists on another course:

> When we teach our children to be gentle, to be forgiving, to be generous, to love their fellow men . . . we instill virtue in their souls and reveal the image of God within them. This then is our task: to educate both ourselves and our children in godliness; otherwise what answer will we have before Christ's judgment seat? . . . How [else] can we be worthy of the kingdom of heaven?[40]

Reclaiming the vision

There exists a great need in the Christian churches today for ecclesial formation, for they stand to become increasingly dissipated if they continue to depend for strength upon cultural supports of Christian faith that are in fact no longer present. The churches must seek ecclesial formation not for their own sake but to prepare believers to greet the Bridegroom when he returns. If Chrysostom was right about the Christian family as a vocation of the kingdom and about the Christian household as a little church, then we would do well in this time and place to reclaim that vision. We must work to make the Christian family once again a training ground in which, by becoming good husbands and wives, fathers and mothers and children, we become "fit to oversee the Church" and good "housekeepers" of God's now and future kingdom.

We also need to join Chrysostom in regarding the church as a body related in various ways to the larger society and reject all notions of the church as an elite group concerned solely with so-called spiritual matters and appropriately heedless of worldly things. Then we will begin to appreciate anew the special value of Chrysostom's vision of the "ecclesial" family for the re-formation of the church and the introduction of a new discipline into its life for the salvation of the world.

9

On Gay Marriage

*I*n pagan Rome during the first centuries of the Christian era, marriage was one of several acceptable forms of cohabitation and family life, and it was available as a legal status only to free citizens. If two such persons, man and woman, lived together in a regularized fashion and assumed the roles and responsibilities of husband and wife, then they were considered legally married. Marriage existed where there was the intention to form a household and did not require legal formalization. The couple could register with the state to qualify for the privileges accorded the institution, including the transmission of the family name to children and the inheritance of the father's estate by legitimate offspring.

There were other acceptable forms of cohabitation. When a freeman cohabited with a slave woman, which was quite common, this was defined legally as concubinage. Roman law stipulated that the essence of marriage was found not in intercourse but in free consent. And since, from the standpoint of custom and law, a slave could not give free consent, a union of freeman and slave woman simply could not be regarded as a marriage. Concubinage did not have the legal benefits of marriage and was therefore less popular. Nevertheless, it was regarded as a respectable estate, and the bearing of children within a concubinal relationship was accepted.

Thus, in this period of the early Roman Empire—let us say the second century—it was acceptable to beget children outside of marriage with no special social stigma attached. For men, neither did extramarital sex before marriage or even within marriage carry a social stigma, though it most certainly did within the church. Divorce was easily obtained. There was considerable tolerance of homosexual behavior, and abortion and infanticide were practiced widely (abortion might be instigated by men to prevent the births of illegitimate offspring, while infanticide was practiced to ensure healthy children and heirs). The church, on the other hand, condemned homosexual behavior, abortion, and infanticide from the beginning.

To this day, Western Christian understandings of marriage continue to reflect the Roman principle of consent. This consensual view of marriage became predominant in Latin and Western Christianity as the church ingested Roman law. The principle of consent contributed to the doctrine of the Roman Catholic Church that the bride and groom are the ministers of the sacrament, that they therefore marry each other; whereas the Eastern Orthodox churches insist that the church marries the bride and groom through the officiation of the clerical celebrant, who in his person represents Christ. This significant difference between Western and Eastern Christian conceptions of marriage is hardly known, understood, or even considered within contemporary debates concerning marriage. But it should be.

Most North Americans who regard themselves as Christian, and many who profess no particular religion at all, simply assume that the consent of the couple lies at the heart of marriage, whether or not marriage is conceived as a contract, a covenant, or a blessing conferred by the church. It is certainly clear that the Roman legal principle of free consent was not without great benefit in the history of Western culture; for example, it opened the way for the liberation of women from near-slave status. But it is this same principle that has allowed support for gay or single-sex marriage to gain momentum in our late-modern context. In the Protestant churches, marriage is not viewed as a sacrament at all, but rather as a solemnized legal contract or a simple blessing that the church confers upon a couple that consent and promise to live together as husband and wife under law. Thus, when vast numbers of people, even within the churches, no longer view homosexual acts as sinful, then the argument that gay marriage ought to be legitimized flows quite easily. When two gay persons desire and freely consent to share their lives with one another as a domestic couple, this argument goes, the state should grant this partnership marital status under civil law, and the church, which loves all its children, should solemnize that marriage. As was once the case with women, a great advance will take place. The freedom of gay and lesbian persons will be expanded. Those who choose to live together in a domestic household will be treated at last with full justice under the equal protection clause of the United States Constitution and receive all the benefits granted to married heterosexual couples and their families.

That is the logic and I doubt that it can be stopped within the present cultural milieu, especially given the impetus of constitutional law. I believe this mounting challenge to the traditional understanding of marriage is emblematic of the crossroads at which our culture stands and which the essays in this book chronicle.

A decade ago, I wrote a book titled *Ethics After Christendom,* in which I endeavored to define the meaning of that very formulation "After Christendom." Therein I offered recommendations for how Christian ethics should be conducted from here on. But I must confess that I did not anticipate that the accelerating cultural and legal dismantlement of the last vestiges of the old Christendom might entail also the disestablishment of the institution of marriage, as it has been known for millennia and was given to us by biblical faith.

It is evident that powerful forces are seeking to depose monogamous heterosexual marriage from its privileged position in our civil code. In the summer of 2004, the United States Senate refused to pass a constitutional amendment that would have defined marriage as consisting strictly of the union between a man and a woman. The House of Representatives responded by passing a measure that was designed to block the federal courts from ordering states to recognize gay marriage sanctioned by other states. In the election of November 2004, citizens of eleven states voted overwhelmingly in favor of amendments to their state constitutions that defined marriage as strictly between a man and a woman. Yet soon afterwards, the United States Supreme Court refused to strike down the Massachusetts Supreme Court's decision legalizing gay marriage in that state.

These were significant skirmishes in a broader cultural struggle that is likely to continue for a long while. Nonetheless, I am inclined to think that eventually, probably under court decree, alternative arrangements for first civil unions and then civil marriages—the two are for all practical purposes indistinguishable—will supplant traditional marriage. We will probably also witness the introduction of polygamous unions, as some Muslims and Mormons demand that right under the equal protection clause. This will constitute the "disestablishment" of the notion that authentic marriage exists only between a man and a woman.

I leave it to others more knowledgeable than I to discuss and debate these legal and political prospects. Here my principal concerns are religious and theological and, therefore, also cultural. I am speaking not only as a Christian theologian, but also as an Orthodox churchman, for I believe that within the religious treasury of Eastern Christianity are a theology of marriage and historical experiences useful to the contemporary debate.

In North America, where Protestant and Roman Catholic Christianity have dominated, persons of biblical faith must start to think not only in post-Christendom terms but also begin to exercise their religious and moral imaginations in "strange" ways with which the Orthodox tradition is more familiar. At this cultural moment, Christians in North America are in a difficult and treacherous situation that calls for careful study and nimble negotiation. Wisdom is needed, perhaps as much wisdom as in that era commencing with Theodosius I (Roman emperor from 379–95) and Theodosius II (emperor from 408–50) and extending through the reign of Justinian (527–65). For during this period of some 150 years, Christianity became the official religion of the empire and the great codes were promulgated that defined and shaped Christendom. This has been our legacy until today, when the heart and spirit of Christendom are once and for all being banished from North American ground and the last of those codes that supported sanctions against abortion, rape, and suicide and permitted public prayer and observation of Christian holy days are cleansed from the land.

A colleague and prominent professor of law at a major university in the South who specializes in family law recently reminded me that Orthodox Christians, especially those with the memory of—and living ties to—the Middle East, have valuable experience that is crucially relevant to the crisis in the meaning and practice of marriage in North America. Arrangements that defined Christian existence under the Ottoman millet system and that persist in variant forms even today in many Middle Eastern countries can serve as models here for new systems of church governance and legal relations with the state. For these churches of Greek, Syrian, and Armenian background have lived and in some places continue to live under arrangements in which civil marriage and religious marriage are clearly distinguished in law and practice. These churches have the historical perspective and the theological resources to help us navigate a different course here in North America.

In the spring of 2004, I delivered a keynote address to the annual diocesan meeting of the Eastern Prelacy of the Armenian Church of America. In that address, I proposed that our bishops instruct priests to withdraw from the standard processes and not deliver marriage consecration on behalf of states that sanction or recognize gay marriage—in simple terms, that they not sign state marriage certificates. I argued that it may no longer be possible or permissible for Armenian clergy in Massachusetts, and no doubt sooner or later in other states, to cooperate or collaborate with the government in marrying persons, as has been carried on in one form or another within Christendom since the fifth and sixth centuries.

Such action would bring about a de facto two-tiered arrangement in which Christians obtain a civil marriage to meet legal requirements and to qualify for married status in the eyes of the state, and then come to the church to receive true, sacramental marriage. Even under present practices, in most states two marriage certificates are issued, one religious and the other civil. Henceforth, the church would no longer assume responsibility for consecration of the civil contract. By taking such action, the church would lodge its profound disagreement with the state's unilateral and theologically mistaken redefinition of marriage.

This ad hoc two-tiered system would be transitional, until such time in which the churches straighten out their ecclesiastical houses sufficiently so that they can manage internally, within the ecclesial body, marriage and all that attends to that institution, including divorce. Churches might then propose to the individual states a separate religious marriage that civil authorities would recognize but over which they would have limited jurisdiction, restricted mainly to guaranteeing basic civil liberties.

I realize that this strategy will seem strange to some churches whose history is different from that of my own confession. Liberal-minded Christians may be inclined to endorse gay marriage as the next step in the progress of Christianity and to register their respect for the autonomy of the state and pluralism. They may not consider the possibility that the outcome will not be pluralism but rather a uniform secularism. Some conservative-minded Christians may cling to the belief that that emulsion of church and society, which constituted Christendom, still exists. Others may concede that it is no longer an emulsion but a suspension, yet continue to hope that, by vigorously shaking the contents, the emulsion can be reconstituted from the separated elements.

I believe that these contending outlooks and strategies are profoundly mistaken and bad for the churches. With the tidal shift in civil law's definition of marriage that is on the horizon, Christian self-identity is at risk. Nevertheless, there might be a hidden silver lining in this development. For the churches have been given an opportunity to recapture the full religious significance of marriage that was lost sight of in late modernity due to entanglements with a state that had become completely secular.

That, in any case, is how this Orthodox Christian theologian sees these matters. Yet such an assertion requires some explanation of the Orthodox theology of marriage. For Western Christians—Roman Catholics and Protestants alike—the essence of marriage has been conceived as the freely given consent of bride and groom, husband and wife. But in the Orthodox tradition this is not so, although the church highly regards human freedom. One looks in vain to find in the Byzantine (Greek) rite of holy matrimony, for example, the familiar exchange of vows. And in all Eastern rites where this ritual does exist, it is a late addition under the influence of Roman law and Latin Christianity. In any case, this exchange of vows belongs to the betrothal service that over the centuries was joined to the crowning ceremony.

In Orthodox Christianity, rather, the conjugal union is the heart of marriage and this union does not depend merely upon the consent of the parties. It is founded in the will of God and effected by an act of God through the sacrament of marriage. Its dimension is not merely temporal but eschatological; its "body" is not merely contractual, or even covenantal, but ecclesial, Christological, and Trinitarian.

In the Armenian rite this conjugal union is indicated by three key actions: the joining of the hands of bride and groom at the beginning of the service, the crowning of the couple, and the sharing of the common cup. By joining the hands of the couple and by the accompanying prayer, the celebrant recalls God's creation of the first couple, Adam and Eve, as "one flesh" (Genesis 2:23). Marriage heals and restores the unsullied and perfect communion of male and female that existed before the ancestral sin and fall brought alienation and discord between the sexes. This is a mystical, sacramental, and eschatological event. An ancient practice of exchanging baptismal crosses, now sadly fallen into disuse, points back to baptism as a calling to discipleship. The crowning of the couple that follows in the rite points to membership in the kingdom of God.

Every marriage is, as St. John Chrysostom explains, a small church in which the virtues of the kingdom are learned and rehearsed. The bride and groom are king and queen of the new heavenly kingdom that is coming into being, as they are called upon also to practice that form of dominion over the world that God intended for the first couple. The crowning looks not merely to the kingdom of God, however. It is also a reminder that the kingdom is gained only through self-giving and self-sacrificial love, as Christ demonstrated when he went willingly to the Cross. Here, then, is the ascetical and martyrial significance of the crowning ceremony.

The sharing of the common cup recalls Jesus' blessing of the wedding in Cana. The water changed to wine is the sign that marriage "in the Lord," as St. Paul puts it, is a sacrament of the kingdom of God. "Natural" marriage is revealed as the matter of that sacrament. Sharing the wine is emblematic of the one-flesh union and life of mutual love to which husband and wife aspire. This practice of the shared cup and the remembered events at Cana allude to Baptism and Eucharist. Thus marriage, like these other two sacraments, is a means by which persons become members of the Body of Christ and participants in the divine life (2 Peter 1:4).

Before all else, Christian marriage is marriage "in the Lord." Christian marriage belongs in its very essence to divine life from all eternity. This is because Jesus Christ, the eternal Son of God, who freely and willingly submitted to crucifixion and death on the Cross for love of the world, is also, as the seer of the Book of Revelation proclaims, "the Lamb slain from the foundation of the world" (Rev.12: 11). He is slain in order that this fallen world might one day be reconciled to God in and through the church. In order that this might be so, Christ is the Groom of the Bride, the church.

In his letter to the Christians of Ephesus, St. Paul writes, "We are members of His body, of His Flesh and of His bones. *'For this reason a man shall leave his father and mother, and be joined to his wife and the two shall become one flesh'* (my emphasis)." Then he adds: "This is a great mystery, but I am speaking concerning Christ and the church" (Eph. 5:30–32). What does Paul mean but that the essence of marriage belongs to the very being of God as unitive love, reflected in everything that God has done to woo Israel to him and all that he is doing to make the church a fitting Bride of Christ?

Orthodox Christianity reads the Bible as enabling the church to say that God has intended from all eternity that she and Christ should be united as Bride and Groom so that the world might be saved from sin and death. Christian marriage is a sign and foretaste of a world reconciled in Christ to God. This is no mere analogy, but belongs to the deepest symbolism that God has built into the fabric of his creation. God created and constituted man and woman as complementary beings who in union constitute a single humanity, a single Adam-Eve existence. In marriage, man-and-woman-together is a sacramental sign of the union of Christ and the church. And God also has made this love-union of man and woman procreative, so that in and through their mutual self-giving, mother, father, and child may begin to learn, image, and experience, even on earth, the triune life of God, the perfectly shared and communicated love of the Father, the Son, and the Holy Spirit.

Within North American society today, these profound Christian truths about the divine and saving character of marriage are contradicted in destructive and disdainful ways. During the spring of 2004, this ignorance of or rejection of Christian truth spilled over into the streets of San Francisco and Boston. Christians need to answer strongly and firmly this attack on the meaning of marriage, not for the sake of what might at best be only short-term victories in the legislatures and courts, but as an earnest testimony of their faith in the love of God and God's holiness.

The early church found no need to perform a special ritual for marriage. Rather, it recognized the legal validity of marriage performed by the civil authorities and invited couples to share the Eucharist together as a sign of their union in Christ and commitment as a couple to the kingdom of God. It was not until the ninth and tenth centuries that a full rite of matrimony emerged. At this time, marriage was removed from the Eucharist, which was replaced by the sharing of the common cup.

Today, the reasons why the church separated marriage from the Eucharist are of great significance and equally instructive. But these reasons have also the bitter taste of a strong irony. In the ninth century, Leo VI (emperor from 886–912) mandated that all marriages henceforth be sanctioned by a church ceremony. A marriage that was not blessed by the church would "not be considered as marriage," but as illegitimate concubinage. Some received this gesture as a great achievement toward the complete Christianization of the empire. Canon 15 of the Armenian Synod of Dvin that met in 719 required compulsory ecclesiastical marriage nearly two centuries before Leo VI's decree. It stated that "the priest ... [should] lead those who are to be crowned into the church and ... conduct over them the order and canon according to Christian regulations." Such promulgations, whether in Armenia or elsewhere in the empire, entailed serious matters of church discipline. And they forced compromises upon the church that ultimately blurred the distinction between religious and secular and between marriage as a legal contract and marriage as a sacrament for baptized believers. Christians have been living with these compromises for over a thousand years for better and for worse (pun intended).

There was one compromise the church could not and would not make, however, lest it forfeit completely its identity as the Body of Christ in the world. That was the admission of nonbelievers, the unbaptized, and known sinners to the Eucharist. In order to mitigate this problem, the church developed a rite of matrimony separate from the Eucharist. It is only since Vatican II, for instance, that the Roman Catholic Church has reinstated a voluntary inclusion of marriage ceremonies within the Eucharistic liturgy.

The moment has now arrived, however, when all churches would do well to rejoin marriage and the Eucharist (or Lord's Supper), precisely in order to protect and preserve the integrity of marriage. The Eucharist is the "home" of Christians. And it is the "home" of Christian marriage as well. The early Christian apologists, who fully acknowledged the legal validity of civil marriage, insisted upon this unbreakable connection between Christian marriage and the Eucharist. Listen to the second-century writer Tertullian, who wrote in a letter to his wife, "What words can describe the happiness of that marriage which the church unites, the [Eucharistic] offering strengthens [i.e., confirms], the blessing seals, the angels proclaim, and the Father declares valid. . . . What a bond is this: two believers who share one hope, one desire, one discipline, the same service."

Clearly, marriage is not fundamentally about civil liberties. Civil liberties, however noble, are proximate goods and do not pertain to our immortal destiny: marriage does. Nor is the American Constitution the constitution of the kingdom of heaven. As a theologian and churchman, I am bound to say that Christ is the constitution of the kingdom, above all other constitutions. Jesus Christ, the Incarnate Son of God, not only spoke the beatitudes to the multitude on the Mount but also lived these virtues perfectly for the sake of all humankind in his representative humanity. Christ is the character of the kingdom as regards its excellence, beauty, goodness, and living truth. The norm and goal of Christian marriage is no less than the holiness God has prescribed, not what some men and women may desire as rights or what the state declares to be legal.

In these times, Christians must eat ever so much more eagerly at Christ's holy Table and on his precious, healing, and life-saving body and blood. A Christian marriage must be no less than a feast at that Table. "Let us be glad and rejoice and give Him glory for the marriage of the Lamb has come, and his wife has made herself ready. . . . 'Blessed are those who are called to the marriage supper of the Lamb'" (Rev. 19:7, 9).

Sometimes the children of God need to be wise as the serpent. Christians must look ahead to a day when in the United States and elsewhere attempts might be made to take marriage back from the church completely and place it firmly in the hands of a secular state. The United States Constitution contains a clause guaranteeing the free exercise of religion. One day, all of the churches might need to lean on it heavily to keep and defend holy marriage. The best position from which to do so will rest in the claim that Christian marriage is entirely integral to Christian worship and is a Eucharistic feast.

In a homily on St. Paul's Letter to the Colossians, St. John Chrysostom exclaims: "The gift of God, the root of the generation is insulted. This then let us cleanse away with our discourse. I am desirous of having marriage purified, so as to bring it back again to its proper nobleness, so as to stop the mouths of the heretics." This expresses what a profound and serious matter a correct understanding of marriage is for the church.

St. Theodore the Studite, in the ninth century, makes mention of two elements that belonged to Eucharistic marriage as early as the fourth century. He informs us that a crowning ceremony existed, followed by a brief prayer. This prayer is virtually replicated at the start of the Armenian rite of marriage. It states: "Thyself, O Master, send down Thy hand from Thy holy dwelling place and unite these Thy servant and Thy handmaid. And give to those whom thou unitest harmony of minds; crown them into one flesh; make their marriage honorable; keep their bed undefiled; deign to make their common life blameless."

Here the whole meaning of Christian marriage is encapsulated. It is God who marries man and woman, and God is present at every Christian marriage. Christian marriage is a sacrament. It is a holy institution and divine calling to discipleship. And through marriage God opens up the gates of the kingdom of heaven to man and woman in their one-flesh union, as God made them and intended for them to be when in the beginning he placed them in the garden of delight.

Now listen to that portion of the Armenian rite of matrimony that immediately follows the hymn of betrothal, when the bride and groom face one another to receive the priestly blessing. They stand facing each other as two complementary presences of one humanity, once divided and now to be reunited by God. With his own hand, the priest joins the right hands of the bride and groom. Then he states: "God took the hand of Eve and gave it into the right hand of Adam. And Adam said: This is bone of my bones and flesh of my flesh.... Wherefore them that God has joined together, let no man separate...." And he continues: "See my dear children in Christ, according to the divine command and the ordinances of the holy fathers of the church, you have come to this holy church in order to be crowned and wedded in holy matrimony. May God keep you in mutual love, lead you to a ripe old age, and make you worthy of the incorruptible crown in heaven...."

Can it be right for a priest of the Armenian Church to use this very same hand with which, as a minister of God, he joins bride and groom in holy matrimony, to sign a license of marriage for a state that has impiously and unilaterally redefined the meaning of that act into something it is not and to its utter defilement? This is a question over which I have prayed and pondered. And I, in conscience, have to say, "It cannot be so!"

10

The Virgin and the Ivy

Above the antique mantel was displayed
As though a window gave up the sylvan scene
The change of Philomel, by the barbarous king
So rudely forced; yet there the nightingale
Filled all the desert with inviolable voice
And still she cried, and still the world pursues,
"Jug Jug" to dirty ears.

— T. S. Eliot, *The Wasteland*

*I*n the ethics course I teach at my college I cover medical ethical issues such as abortion, euthanasia, reproductive technologies, and care for the dying. I also include a section on sexuality and marriage. For the past several years, I have assigned a book written by a young woman, Wendy Shalit, that was published two years after she graduated from Williams College in 1997. *A Return to Modesty: Discovering the Lost Virtue* is a report on sex and today's college student. Shalit describes the pressure on young women who choose to remain chaste in college, and she recommends strategies for living by more traditional sexual standards. Predictably, the book has been praised by conservative reviewers and mocked by liberal commentators. It is not a perfect book and certainly can be faulted for overgeneralizing and for indulging in a facile journalistic style pervasive in popular trade publishing today. Nevertheless, *A Return to Modesty*'s snapshot report of sex on campus—how it is perceived and pursued by Shalit's peers—rings true.

My students generally agree that Shalit's descriptions of dormitory life and contemporary dating practices are accurate; my son and daughter, both recent college graduates, say the same. I attended college in the late sixties when institutions of higher learning summarily surrendered the responsibilities of *in loco parentis* and opened the floodgates to the so-called sexual revolution, inviting much of what goes on today in college dormitories and beds. So I am not altogether surprised by what my students tell me or what Shalit reports. Still, like so many parents and teachers, I suppose I have sought comfort, or at least some modicum of peace of mind, by not asking these young people: "Tell me. What really goes on?"

Of late I *have* asked that question, however. I suppose I have done so in no small measure because I have begun to see my students as my own children. I know that young people are getting hurt, some permanently scarred for life, and I hold colleges like my own morally accountable, if not complicit in this harm. The colleges know what is going on and they keep their mouths shut, running for shelter behind bogus appeals to personal autonomy and privacy and shoveling out self-serving rhetoric about respecting college students as adults. And when those "adults" get hurt, they order up more psychologists and therapists to bandage the casualties, my children and yours.

An instructive tale

Though my own specific concern and experience is in the university setting, I want to begin by telling the story of some events that transpired several years ago not at a college but at a highly respected preparatory school in Baltimore. At the end of March in that year, the local news media reported that some young men at St. Paul's School for Boys, most of them on the nationally top-ranked lacrosse team, had either been implicated in videotaping a friend having sex with a young woman or later viewed that video at a private residence. Within days the Board of Trustees and Headmaster Robert W. Hallett announced the suspension or expulsion of the young men involved. Significantly, he also canceled the varsity lacrosse season.

Hallett's actions were swift, severe, and consistent with the high standards of a one-hundred-and-fifty-year-old Episcopal school that is proud of its Honor System—one of the oldest in the nation—and its commitment to the moral and intellectual cultivation of young men. In his prepared remarks to parents on April 3, 2001, Hallett did not mince words about the nature of the young men's behavior and the harm they had done to the young woman. "It is an understatement," he said, "to say this is a devastating event—first and foremost because a young woman was humiliated. . . . Some of our students I know have made personal expressions of apology to her, and I believe more will and should be forthcoming. . . . In a real sense this will never be over or finished. The educational 'takeaways' will last a lifetime. At minimum we should expect each boy here will, in the future, have the courage to stand up for, to quote the Lower School prayer, 'The hard right against the easy wrong.'" Hallett concluded his remarks by stating, "When I addressed the student body last Friday, I spoke of confession, atonement, and redemption. We heard confession; we now seek atonement in the hope that by God's grace we can gain redemption."

I quote these words with pride as the parent of an alumnus of St. Paul's School for Boys. Headmaster Robert W. Hallett's was an all-too-rare display of Christian courage, conviction, and leadership in American education. The St. Paul's School for Boys' reputation suffered considerably during the month that this scandal gripped the attention of the media and the public. The school's integrity, however, was saved because the Headmaster and Board of Trustees faced squarely the challenge.

Yet what of the integrity of other schools and colleges where such things undoubtedly go on but are kept quiet? As a parent of one of the St. Paul's School lacrosse players commented to a *Baltimore Sun* reporter: "Trust me. Every coach in this town is on the ground kissing it because it could have happened anywhere."

As the St. Paul's controversy swirled in the media, I found my thoughts occupied by the following brutally and painfully honest exposé of the sexual environment at my college written by one of my students. In her response to reading *A Return to Modesty*, this young woman also reported on practices at another college attended by her boyfriend—behavior disturbingly similar to what was revealed at St. Paul's School for Boys.

> My boyfriend has told me stories about his fraternity brothers who have "Showtime at the Apollo." This is when a guy knows that he is going to bring a girl home and tells his friends. He then leaves the curtain to the glass door of the dual access balcony cracked so that his friends can sit on the balcony and watch. He then proceeds to humiliate the girl in front of his friends. Now my boyfriend's defense of his brothers is that any girl who will allow you to sleep with her the first night, and doesn't leave after you begin to do such degrading sexual acts, deserves it. And she never finds out anyway. My brother has concurred with him stating, "You only treat a girl like a slut, if she is a slut."

These times, they are a-changin'

What is available to the carnal and prurient imagination has certainly expanded since my undergraduate days at the University of Virginia. I can say with complete confidence that my fraternity brothers would never have conceived or executed such a scheme in voyeurism—and believe me, there were rogues among those fellows. But today, behavior like what happened at St. Paul's School or what was described by this young coed are depicted in the cinema and regularly jested about on primetime television sitcoms and talk shows.

When I entered the University of Virginia in 1966—it was then still an all-men's college—the rules were clear: no women in the dorm rooms or beyond the public spaces in fraternity houses. These rules had objective force. They were not left to the individual to decide. And these rules were enforced by students, with lapses to be sure, but enforced nonetheless, if for no other reason than the school expected it. As for the young women who visited from the many neighboring women's colleges, *in loco parentis* as embraced by their schools stipulated that they secure approved housing so that—if they wanted to—they could gracefully say "No" to the advances of their dates and make it stick. Of course there were private apartments, cheap hotels, and cow pastures beyond the pale of *in loco parentis*. Still, all in all, rules and institutional arrangements with real sanctions established the boundaries of acceptable behavior.

This made for a vastly different college culture than exists today at the University of Virginia or Loyola College. But I am no newcomer—I was "at the revolution." Within three short years after my arrival at the University of Virginia, the old regime was swept completely aside and my fraternity brothers and their girlfriends commenced their descent into today's Brave New World of student and dormitory life. It's no accident that I begin my ethics course with Aldous Huxley's novel. And no small number of students remark that there is an unsettling similarity between college dormitory life and *Brave New World*, where promiscuity is a virtue, virginity as unspeakable a word as motherhood, and monogamous fidelity a sin against society. My students do not maintain that this environment is unique to college, only that because the sexes are brought together in closed quarters, almost hermetically sealed off from parents, teachers, and the rest of society, there is every incentive and great pressure to pursue the "experiment." As one young woman exclaimed in class, "Here we can do everything we were told at home was wrong, and no one really cares, and no one is responsible. It's like we live in a glass bubble, only no one can look in."

Another young woman elaborated on the resemblance between Huxley's fictional world and college life. In *Brave New World*, Lenina Crowne breaks the unwritten code against dating one person exclusively and is chided by her roommates for doing so:

> "But seriously," [Fanny] said, "I really do think you ought to be careful. It's such horribly bad form to go on and on like this with one man. At forty, or thirty-five it wouldn't be so bad. And you know how the D.H.C. [Director of Hatcheries and Conditioning] objects to anything intense or long-drawn. Four months of Henry Foster, without having another man, why he'd be furious if he knew."

This student comments:

> The terms dating and love bring on a whole new meaning in Huxley's novel. Promiscuity is required, while being with the same person for too long a time is shunned. "Everyone belongs to everyone else" is the motto, and for Lenina this is an issue. She's been seeing the same man . . . for a long time . . . and people are starting to wonder. . . . Lenina says herself that she "hadn't been feeling very keen on promiscuity lately. . . ." *It seems as if many girls are feeling the same pressure today* [my emphasis]. According to Shalit, sex isn't being treated as a big deal anymore, so many [young people] are doing it because they feel it is expected of them to remain sexually healthy. It is as if Huxley saw this type of society coming where sleeping around is accepted and encouraged. . . . For example, a woman

today who wants to wait until marriage to have sex has to experience a lot of turmoil and anguish from [members] of the opposite sex who do not want a virgin. This is best put by Shalit when she writes, "To the extent that premarital sex is practiced and encouraged, to that extent will women who want to wait until marriage find it harder to meet men who will marry without 'trying them out' first . . . , [and] have patience with 'hang ups'—which is to say 'hopes.'"

Let us not confuse the young woman who wrote this with the real or imagined traditional Catholic girl of a generation or two ago. I am constantly surprised by the wisdom of the serpent and not the innocence of the dove in such young women. They have had to learn how to "survive" in a dangerous and hostile environment. It is not that the young men they meet at college are necessarily less moral than the fellows with whom I went to college. It is, rather, that these young men know they can force matters further because the rules and institutional safeguards under which young women once upon a time could take protective cover are gone. Let us not kid ourselves: *Coed dorms and apartments work to the advantage of male sexual aggression at the expense of female modesty.*

Hooking up

So just what goes on at colleges and universities like my own, and what impact do contemporary social-sexual practices have on young men and women, especially women? I defer to the young coed whom I cited earlier regarding the behavior of her boyfriend's fraternity brothers. She writes: "Before I drop my roommates off at the bar tonight, they will drink as they primp themselves in hopes that they will bring home someone to spend the night." Dating in the traditional sense, which still resembled what was once called courtship, is a passing if not purely anachronistic

139

social custom. "Hooking up" is what these roommates are after. In *A Return to Modesty,* Shalit cites a book about contemporary dating and sexual habits of college students which describes "hooking up."

> You . . . [are] almost certainly acting on physical attraction, not a well-formed emotional attachment, and there . . . [is] no risk to either of you. You're under no obligation to date each other or call each other—nor should you expect to be called or dated. . . . [I]f you realize almost immediately after you finish sex that this will be a one-time event and really don't want to pursue any relationship, even a purely physical one, with this person, try not to sleep through the night with the person. . . . Leaving someone with whom you've traded bodily fluids can seem strange, rude, and inconsiderate, but at least you'll have the knowledge that you were being honest. . . .

At Loyola the hook-up is accommodated with what this young woman identifies as the "booty room." "We have a designated 'booty room,'" she writes, "for the purpose of being alone with one of these boys [picked up at a bar] and not disturbing your immediate roommate." Traditional "boyfriend" and "girlfriend" terms still apply, but they have been expanded to differentiate between sex that is solely recreational and sex that may entail a commitment of some sort. Boyfriend-girlfriend sex is of an order other than sex that is occasioned by the "hook-up"—sex an earlier generation called "the one-night stand." But the lines can blur because the rules are made up as you go along. This young woman explains how she negotiated boyfriend-girlfriend status with her love interest:

> I . . . told my boyfriend that he needed to ask me to be his girlfriend because I wasn't going to be "that girl" who just assumed boyfriend status. This is because you can never assume that he has become your boyfriend, even after

continuous hook-ups, phone calls, and even sex. The "booty room" has been used many times, but not by those with a boyfriend, but by roommates who don't have someone with them regularly. As for the two of us, it's just fine that all four of us [the young woman, her boyfriend, her roommate, and her roommate's boyfriend] sleep in the same room.

A smoldering wick in the tempest

I have said that I am constantly surprised not by the dove-like innocence of such young women at Loyola College but by the worldly wisdom that they have learned in order to navigate a course of integrity and relative purity in the sordid environment of dormitory life. Just as encounters in the "booty room" may not lead to sexual intercourse, so cohabitation in dorm rooms may not necessarily entail coitus. Despite the fact this young woman sleeps in the same room with her boyfriend, she has remained a virgin. She thoughtfully explains what lies behind her commitment:

> First of all, I was raised that sex before marriage was not appropriate. The influence of my older brother was significant. He did all he could so that I would not be one of those "sluts." The fact that my best friend is quite promiscuous, and I have to hear people talk poorly about her, does not make the option appealing. But most of all, I think my decision has to do with a bad experience that I had.

She continues,

> I had a boyfriend when I was "young and naïve" who told me that the only way to get him back was to sleep with him. And

> I almost did. I later realized that I was in some irrational state
> of mind and I could have given up something that I believe in
> because of a person who didn't love me.

As certain as this young woman is about having made the right decision, she still fears that in the future she may not be able to muster the strength to stay the course. She ponders what awaits her after college when close friendships with young men and women of like beliefs may be few and the support system to live a sexually "modest" life weakened even further. What if after college "my current, understanding boyfriend and I were to split, would I be able to have a healthy relationship without sleeping with anyone? I used to think, who will want me if I do? Now I think, who will want me if I don't?"

Forsaking a trust, undermining a calling

The college dormitory, like the modern college itself, has its origins in the Christian monastery. We have come a long way. Far from being a place dedicated to self-discipline and hospitable to reflective study, the modern college dormitory is a playground of recreational sex and post-Christian cohabitation. We must not underestimate the deleterious and debilitating impact of this kind of living on moral formation and the quality of human relationships among college students. "Book-learning" is also affected. The kind of life my students live outside of the classroom has an immediate negative bearing upon their ability to study and learn. These things are related, character and education, living and learning. Loyola College affirms as much in its school motto: "Strong truths well lived." Present conditions contradict this ideal and render it an empty platitude.

Lest it be overlooked, what happened to St. Paul's School was the result of activity beyond the school's jurisdiction, in private homes. And still the school took full responsibility because St. Paul's School believes that truth, morality, and education are intrinsically related and cannot be divided or compartmentalized without doing serious harm to human personality and human relations. What happens among students at Loyola College is in school-owned and -supervised dormitories and apartments. To be sure, Loyola College is not alone among institutions of higher education in its inattention to the total environment of student life. It is no more an unhealthy place to be than most colleges today. But Loyola College's mission statement says that it is "dedicated to the ideals of liberal education and *cura personalis*" (care of the whole human being). And the college claims a relationship to a church that maintains, among other things, a high view of marriage and sexual union.

Prescinding from an immediate judgment about the sexual practices of these students considered in themselves, it is clear that the experiences to which these young people are subjecting themselves while at Loyola College will have a significant and pernicious impact on their future relationships and marriages. Statistics are unambiguous—they show that first marriages that begin with cohabitation are far more likely to end in divorce or dissolution than other marriages.

The failure of America's institutions of higher education—especially Christian ones—is not merely administrative. It is a failure of vision and a failure of loyalty to their religious and educational missions. When students are learning all the wrong habits in their daily college lives, how can a truly humanistic higher learning occur? How can I teach Christian ethics with force and effect in the classroom when my college will not address or remedy the degrading living conditions my students have described? How can I possibly speak with authority as a moral theologian in such an environment?

In the meantime the virgin perishes in the ivy and it is my professional and personal agony to hear her plaintive cry. "'Jug Jug' to dirty ears."

11

Dorm Brothel

"The so-called sexual revolution is not, as advertised, a liberation of sexual behavior but rather its reversal. In former days, even under Victoria, sexual intercourse was the natural end and culmination of heterosexual relations. Now one begins with genital overtures instead of a handshake, then waits to see what will turn up (e.g., might become friends later). Like dogs greeting each other nose to tail and tail to nose."

— Walker Percy, *The Last Gentleman*

N ineteen sixty-six, the year in which Walker Percy's *The Last Gentleman* was published, is also the year I entered as a First-Year Man at the University of Virginia. We did not stoop to the State U level of referring to ourselves as freshmen, sophomores, and such—not at "The University." We were all men at U. Va.: "gentlemen," we were told. Young women visited on weekends from Sweet Briar and Randolph-Macon, Mary Washington and Hollins College. But they did not stay in the dormitory or the fraternity house. They stayed in college-approved housing, more often than not the home of a widow who had a few rooms to let and happily accepted a delegation from the colleges to assume the responsibilities of *in loco parentis.* Parietal rules were enforced even in the fraternity houses—self-enforced by those of us who lived in them. Young women were not permitted in the bedrooms and had to be out of the house by a certain hour. We dated, blind-dated often. We did not know what "hooking up" was. We had never heard of date rape, either, though some of us may have committed it. It could happen in the backseat of a car, a cheap motel, a cow pasture, or a Civil War battlefield, but not in a college dormitory or fraternity house bedroom, not yet at least; it was not until the end of the decade that all the rules and prohibitions came tumbling down and the brave new world of the contemporary coeducational college commenced.

Back then, and from time immemorial, so far as I knew, there were the "easy" girls. We had a provocative name or two for them and they were quickly sorted out from the "other" girls. Word got around fast. These were not young women one seriously considered marrying, and most of us expected and hoped to find a mate in college. If, however, a guy got especially "hungry" or "horny," there was no special stigma attached to taking advantage of what the easy girls had to offer.

The gentlemen of the University of Virginia lived by a double standard, but there *were* standards. There was little doubt about that. The arrangements the colleges provided for the sexes to meet and mix, strict dorm-visitation hours, approved housing, curfews for female visitors, and the like made that abundantly clear. When we set off on a road trip to a girls school, either by hitchhiking or jamming six or eight into a car, and arrived at the dorm, we did not just mosey on up to our dates' rooms and hang out. We waited, garbed in coat and tie, in the big informal parlor until our dates made their entrance.

My college classmates and fraternity brothers at the University of Virginia and I were certainly not Victorians, but we were not post-Christian and postmodern young men, either, not quite yet. Maybe we were the *last gentlemen*, which certainly should not be interpreted to mean that we always behaved like gentlemen, just that we had some appreciation for the meaning of the word and maybe even aspirations to become what it signified. Furthermore, we knew what the opposite of a gentleman was. In fact, in those days, "The University" was often called, proudly by some, the Playboy School of the South. So we were gentleman and play-boys both, spirited by our friend Jack Daniels. We knew that there was a contradiction in being a gentleman and a Don Juan at the same time. But being a Don Juan or Playboy has significance only in a world in which the idea of the gentleman exists, in which fidelity is acknowledged as a virtue, and in which sex is considered most appropriate to the marital union. We had absorbed these notions from a culture that had not yet abandoned them. We knew the game had to end eventually, probably when we met the right girl and got married, and most of us got married by the age of twenty-three or twenty-four, many to our college sweethearts.

One could say that in 1966 what men and women called dating was a late—and as I look back on it, probably also tenuous—version of court-ship. We understood, at least implicitly, that there was an important dif-ference between going whoring and dating. Treating a young woman like a whore was what a Don Juan would do, but not a gentleman, especially one looking for a future wife. But today is entirely different. My grown children tell me so, as do my students at Loyola College, and much has been written on the subjects of dating, courtship, and the sexual attitudes of our youth that confirms their testimony. But why is dating, as a form of courtship, an endangered practice?

Experts identify a variety of reasons and causes, but I do not pretend to address the subject scientifically or dispassionately. I will not review the literature here. Nor do I have a sentimental attachment to a remem-bered past. Lest I be misunderstood, I do not call for a return to the "good old days" of dating as it was when I was a youth anymore than I would advocate a return to arranged marriages. As a college professor and father of a college-age daughter, however, I am outraged by the complicity of my college and most other schools in the death of courtship and the emer-gence of a dangerous and destructive culture of "hooking up."

Doane College in Nebraska recently mailed a recruiting postcard that showed a man surrounded by women, with a caption that read that students at this college have the opportunity to "play the field." After a public outcry last December, administrators hastily withdrew the marketing campaign, explaining that the postcard was harmless and a metaphor for exploring a variety of educational options. But the very fact that the campaign was conceived and approved in the first place speaks volumes. The sexual revolution, if that is an appropriate title, was not won with guns but with genital groping aided and abetted by colleges that forfeited their responsibilites of *in loco parentis* and have gone into the pimping and brothel business.

Sex carnival

I do not use these words lightly or loosely, and rarely is a college so blatantly suggestive as was Doane, although this attitude about the commendability of sexual experimentation has become an orthodoxy among many who hold positions as deans of student life at our colleges. Of course, some colleges take concrete steps to resist this revolution of morals. Still, in most American college coed dorms, the flesh of our daughters is being served up daily like snack jerky. No longer need young men be wolves or foxes to consume that flesh. There are no fences to jump over or chicken coops to break into. The gates are wide open and no guard dogs have been posted. It is easy come and easy go. Nor are our daughters the only ones getting hurt. The sex carnival that is college life today is also doing great damage to our sons' characters, deforming their attitudes toward the opposite sex. I am witnessing a perceptible dissolution of manly virtue in the young men I teach.

Nevertheless, my more compelling concern about this state of affairs is for the young women, our daughters. Since my student years, colleges have abandoned all the arrangements that society had once put in place to protect the "weaker sex" so they could say "no" and have a place to which to retreat if young men pressed them too far. And although even when these arrangements were in place one could not always say with confidence that the girl was the victim and the boy the offender, the contemporary climate makes identifying predator and prey even trickier. The lure and availability of sexual adventure that our colleges afford is teaching young women also to pursue sexual pleasures aggressively. Yet, based on my own conversations and observations, there is no doubt that young women today are far more vulnerable to sexual abuse and mistreatment by young men than when I was a college student, simply because the institutional arrangements that protected young women are gone and the new climate says everything goes.

In 1966, my fraternity brothers and I were caught up in a monumental shift in relations between the sexes that Will Barrett, the young protagonist of Walker Percy's tale, struggles to understand and come to terms with. One evening, Will and his love interest, Kitty Vaught, retreat to a cramped camper. They try to dance and then lie together in a bunk with all the expectations ignited by young flesh pressed against young flesh. A conversation ensues that is profoundly emblematic of what my generation went through. Prompted by the intimacy and abandon of the situation, Will tells Kitty a story about how his grandfather took his father to a whorehouse at the age of sixteen. Kitty asks Will if his father did the same for him. Will answers that he did not. Then, after some chatter about the meaning of love and the difficulty of it, Kitty says to Will, "Very well, I'll be your whore." Will does not protest, so Kitty injects,

"Then you think I'm a whore?"

"No," That was the trouble. She wasn't. There was a lumpish playfulness, a sort of literary gap in her whorishness.

"Very well, I'll be a lady."

"All right."

"No, truthfully. Love me like a lady."

"Very well."

He lay with her, more or less miserably, kissed her lips and eyes and uttered sweet love murmurings into her ear, telling her what a lovely girl she was. But what am I, he wondered: neither Christian nor pagan nor proper lusty gentleman, for I've never really got the straight of this lady-and-whore business. And that is all I want and it does not seem much to ask: for once and all to get the straight of it.

This is what dating was becoming back then, as young men and women without traditional adult oversight started to entrust themselves to one another. A clear sense of the formal stages of courtship had faded and authoritative rules of conduct were dissolving. Percy's scene is not wholly foreign to my students. But neither is it typical. The culture has changed dramatically.

Literary hook-ups

When, in Tom Wolfe's most recent novel, *I Am Charlotte Simmons,* Charlotte's mother asks her during Christmas break where students go on dates at Dupont University, Charlotte responds, "Nobody goes out on a date. The girls go out in groups and the boys go out in groups, and they hope they find somebody they like." This is Charlotte Simmons's description of "hooking up," which has replaced traditional courtship and dating among today's college students. "Hooking up" is dating sans courtship or expectations of a future relationship or commitment. It is strictly about user sex. I use you and you use me for mutual pleasure. And alcohol is more often than not the lubricant that makes things go.

We all are familiar with contemporary sitcoms and so-called reality television shows that bring young men and women together with precisely the intent of getting them to eye each other's genitals like candy at a convenience store, respond to each other's sexual nature in animal fashion, and hop in bed together with no regrets. There are no evident prohibitions or taboos. The comic or dramatic plot is all about sexual adventure and getting as much pleasure from the experience as possible. The rules are strictly instrumental. Often, they are made up along the way merely to facilitate the smooth going of the "game" or "hunt," as it might more appropriately be called.

I cannot say for sure whether these shows influence real life or whether it is the other way around. In the end, it does not matter much. What I do know is that a latter-day Walker Percy could not write the scene I have cited with the belief that it faithfully depicts how contemporary young men and women meet or what is at issue between them.

Take, for another example, the benchmark movies of the sixties about young men and women coming of age, such as *The Graduate* or Francis Ford Coppola's *You're a Big Boy Now*. They are now passé. The sexual innocence they depict and the presence of adult supervision, limited or mocked, against which the young protagonists struggle, are no longer realistic. Frank Capra's classic romantic comedy *It Happened One Night,* released in 1934, contrasts even more strikingly with contemporary sexual mores. In that movie, a newspaper reporter named Peter Warne, played by Clark Gable, heroically and humorously lives up to the standard of a gentleman in his behavior toward a rebellious young heiress named Ellie Andrews, played by Claudette Colbert. Occasions arise that certainly present Peter with opportunities to make sexual advances. But Peter does not take advantage of these occasions, despite his increasing desire for a woman whom at first he disdained. Only after these two spirited combatants of the war between the sexes get wed is it suggested that they are sexually intimate. At the end of the film, a symbolic trumpet sounds, announcing that the "walls of Jericho" are falling.

Over the years I have asked my students whether they have seen this movie. Only a handful of the students in my course on theology and literature acknowledge even having heard of it. If they were to watch *It Happened One Night,* I do not doubt that some of my students would enjoy it and highly appreciate its artistry and humor. Yet I hardly think many would identify strongly with the characters and their situation. In simple terms, the symbolic curtain that Peter builds from a clothesline and a blanket in order to separate two twin beds in a rented room is hardly the correlative of life in coed college dormitories and apartments today.

The nature and depth of this cultural disconnect is illustrated by a scene in Aldous Huxley's *Brave New World*, published just two years after *It Happened One Night* premiered. John, the so-called Savage, is brought to London from the Indian reservation. During a conversation with Helmholtz Watson, a young author of radio jingles and touchy-feely movie scripts, John recites lines from *Romeo and Juliet*, a play that has been banned and is unknown to the inhabitants of *Brave New World*. Despite the fact that Helmholtz rebels against the shallowness of life in *Brave New World*, the plot of Shakespeare's play puzzles him. After listening to the scene of the lovers' first meeting, he wonders what all the fuss is about. He does not understand the nature of the tragedy because he has no knowledge of courtship or the roles of parental and filial love and fidelity in Shakespeare's world. "Getting into such a state about having a girl—it seemed rather ridiculous. . . . The mother and father (grotesque obscenity) forcing the daughter to have someone she didn't want! And the idiotic girl not saying that she was having some one else whom (for the moment, at any rate) she preferred! In its smutty absurdity the situation was irresistibly comical."

It Happened One Night was made more than three hundred years after Shakespeare wrote his plays. Nevertheless, its humor and ennobling power rest on standards of propriety and courtship nearer to the sixteenth century than to Huxley's futuristic London or even today's hook-up culture. The reading public of the twentieth century's first decades might find the abolition of courtship and marriage in *Brave New World* interesting and remote, but my students readily admit the possibility of such a future. I recently gave a lecture at Loyola on *Brave New World*. During the question-and-answer period, there was a brief discussion about the similarities of dormitory life with *Brave New World*. I opined that whatever the resemblances, there is a clear difference between the two: sexual promiscuity and hooking up among college students is voluntary, I said, whereas in *Brave New World* this behavior is mandatory. A young woman and dormitory resident advisor walked up to me afterwards and chided me: "Dr. Guroian, you are mistaken about that. The peer pressure and the way things are set up make promiscuity practically obligatory. It doesn't matter what the school says officially. The rules are to be broken. This freedom can make girls dizzy and unsure of whatever else they believe about 'saving oneself' for marriage. When it seems like everyone else is 'doing it,' it is hard to say no. It is more like *Brave New World* here than you think. I deal with it or, more frequently, turn my eyes from it, every day as an RA."

During the spring semester, this same young woman, who was enrolled in one of my classes, wrote a brief exposé on what goes on at Loyola College and other colleges. She explains the sundry distinctions today's young men and women make in relationships and sexual liaisons.

> It may not be that dating is at the brink of extinction, but ... it has taken a back seat in the modern-day lives of students. Hooking up, going out, going steady, and dating, contrary to what some may think, are not the same thing. ... If you are "going out" with someone it means that you have a boyfriend or a girlfriend, you are in a "steady" relationship with that person. However, a couple needn't actually go anywhere [go on dates together] to be in this kind of relationship. Hooking up is basically dating without the romance. It has become customary for young adults to simply cut to the chase, the sexual ... part of a relationship. A hook up can be a one-time thing, as it most often is, or it can be a semi-regular thing, but not a full relationship. Although it may take on the signs of one.
>
> One might conclude that modern-day youth has simply gotten lazy and careless. Most ... are not looking for a romantic

relationship; they see the new freedom and plethora of sexual opportunities and simply take what they can get. They get to college and it's an amusement park with so many different enticing rides, one would be missing out on the whole experience to settle with the first one they tried. And why should they bother with the responsibility and formalities of a date when they have a better chance of getting immediate satisfaction after buying a few drinks at a bar?

I could have foregone quoting this young coed to cite any number of studies that describe these phenomena more "scientifically." These studies try hard to be "objective," but as a result they cannot convey the immediacy and passion of this young woman's narrative or the matter-of-fact manner in which she draws connections between the breakdown of courtship, the rise of a hook-up culture, and what we used to call pimping and prostitution. "Co-ed dormitories," she continues, "are they an ideal situation or a sad form of prostitution? You go out with your friends on your terms, after a few drinks you're both attracted. . . . Interested and lonely, you go together, no obligations, no responsibilities, and no rules. Then there is that late night 'booty call.' This has become such a custom of the college lifestyle [that] most have come to accept it, although maybe not respect it. If it were really the ideal situation, the walk home the next day [to one's own room] wouldn't be called 'the walk of shame.'" At Loyola College, the vast majority of students live on campus, and since the college has bought up a number of neighboring high-rise and garden apartments, after the freshman year the "walk of shame" need not even be made. It may be only a few steps from the boy's apartment to the girl's, or better yet, from the boy's *room* to the girl's.

The Culpable College

The campaign against alcohol and drugs, which it seems every American college has proudly announced it is waging, is a smokescreen that covers the colleges' great sin. Regulating a substance like alcohol on an urban campus like Loyola's cannot succeed unless there is radical reform of the whole of college life. Nothing that the college does to limit alcohol consumption can make a significant difference until the major incentives to drink are removed, beginning with coed dormitories and apartments. Many of my students have explained to me that drinking, especially binge drinking, serves as the lubricant for the casual sex that living arrangements at Loyola invite and permit. There is no need to find the cheap hotel of yesterday. The college provides a much more expensive and available version of it.

The sexual adventures that follow can take a variety of paths, but what this young Loyola man describes is not atypical:

> True story: I woke up at three in the morning one day last year to my roommate having sex in his bed five feet away from me. Taking a moment to actually wake up, I realized what was going on. I got up . . . , heard what was going on, and . . . recognized the voice of the girl. . . . I had two classes with her the semester before and one that semester. . . . The next morning . . . there was no awkward exchange. No childish giggling. I simply told him that I could not believe that she didn't mind having sex with someone for the first time while someone else was in the room sleeping. I also couldn't believe that she hadn't stopped and covered herself up when I had walked out of the room. My roommate looked at me with a casual smile, the same smile I'd seen when talking about the Mets or Red Sox, the same smile I'd seen at our dining room

table over Taco Bell, and he said to me, "Whatever, she's a college girl."

This is a disturbing description of the demise of decency and civility between the sexes for which the American colleges are culpable and blameworthy. It is not that what this student describes was unheard of in the 1960s. Frankly, I can tell similar stories about my college experience. Nevertheless, this was the exception rather than a commonplace occurrence. For colleges made it clear to young men and women that such behavior was unacceptable, and had in place living arrangements with rules and sanctions that discouraged it.

There is nothing new or novel about human depravity or debauchery. Outrage over debauchery is deserved. Nevertheless, as I have suggested already, my outcry is not directed at the debauchery among college students, but rather at the colleges themselves. Today, colleges not only turn a blind eye to this behavior, but also set up the conditions that foster and invite it. I am concerned about the young men and women who wish to behave differently, but for whom this is made especially difficult by the living conditions their colleges provide and often insist upon.

In *I Am Charlotte Simmons,* a fictitious counterpart of the young woman and resident advisor whom I cited earlier says to the new freshmen under her supervision, "The university no longer plays the role of parents." She means that sex is permitted. The satiric irony is that there are rules against keeping or consuming alcohol in the dorms. Is that not also *in loco parentis?* Charlotte quickly learns, however, that all of these rules are made to be broken and that being "sexiled," which means being expelled from one's room so that one's roommate may have sex, is routine and obligatory at Dupont University.

In the new culture that our colleges incubate and maintain, everyone is a "guy." Everyone is "familiar." Young men and women who have never seen anyone of the opposite sex naked or in underwear, other than family members, now must get used to being seen by and seeing others—perfect strangers—in just such a state. Everyone is available to everyone else. It would be antisocial not to be.

Under such conditions, how could dating and courtship possibly survive? How could traditional marriage survive in the long term? Courtship and dating require an inviolable private space from which each sex can leave at appointed times to meet in public and enjoy the other. In other words, in a courtship culture it *ought* to be that two people who are "serious" actually do "go out" together and do not merely cohabitate in a closeted dormitory or apartment. Yet over the past forty years, American colleges have created a brave new unisex world in which distinctions between public and private, formal and familiar, have collapsed. The differences between the sexes are now dangerously minimized or else just plain ignored because to recognize them is not progressive or politically correct. This is manifestly the case with coed dorm floors and shared bathrooms and showers. These give the lie to official college rules against cohabitation. They are the wink and nod our colleges give to fornication and dissipation. Even in 1957, when he was chancellor of the University of California at Berkeley, Clark Kerr was almost prophetic when he stated humorously that his job responsibilities were "providing parking for faculty, sex for students, and athletics for the alumni."

Loyola College and a great many other colleges and universities simply do not acknowledge, let alone address, the sexualization of the American college. Rather, they do everything possible to put a smiley face on an unhealthy and morally destructive environment, one that—and this is no small matter—also makes serious academic study next to impossible. Most of the rhetoric one hears incessantly from American colleges about caring for young men and women and respecting their so-called freedom and maturity is disingenuous. Should we really count it to their credit that colleges are spending increasing resources on counseling and therapy when the direct cause of many wounds they seek to heal is the brave new world that they have engineered, sold as a consumer product, and supervised?

To serve *in loco parentis* involves caring for the whole student not as an employer or client but as a parent. In its statement "Vision and Values: A Guide for the Loyola College Community," Loyola says it holds to "an ideal of personal wholeness and integration." The college aims "to honor, care for, and educate the whole person," enjoining the entire college community "to strive after intellectual, physical, psychological, social, and spiritual health and well-being." The statement correctly associates these goals of education with the Roman Catholic faith and the liberal arts tradition. Many other colleges and universities issue similar statements of aim and purpose on both religious and secular grounds. Yet the climate at Loyola College—and many, many others—produces the antithesis of these aims. It fosters not growth into wholeness but the dissolution of personality, not the integration of learning and everyday living but their radical bifurcation. It most certainly does not support the church's values of marriage and family.

Young men and women are being enticed to think of themselves as two selves, one that is mind and reason in the classroom and another self, active "after hours," that is all body and passion. They begin to imagine—though few entirely believe it—that they can use (that is, abuse) their bodies as they please for pleasure, and that choosing to do so has nothing to do with their academic studies or future lives. In reality, they are following a formula for self-disintegration and failure.

This is the grizzly underbelly of the modern American college; the deep, dark, hidden secret that many parents suspect exists but would rather not face. The long-term damage is difficult to measure. But it is too obvious to deny. I remember once hearing that the British lost the empire when they started sending their children away to boarding schools. I do not know whether anyone has ever seriously proposed that thesis. But I am prepared to ask whether America might not be lost because the great middle class was persuaded that they must send their children to college with no questions asked, when in fact this was the near equivalent of committing their sons and daughters to one of the circles of Dante's Inferno.

I have lived long enough to understand and be thankful for the fact that the sins and indiscretions of youth may be forgiven and overcome. The behavior of our American colleges and universities, however, is inexcusable. Their mendacity is doing great harm to our children, whom we entrust to them with so much love, pride, and hope for the future.

12

Huxley's Mirror

The theme of *Brave New World* is not the advancement of science as such; it is the advancement of science as it affects human individuals. ... The only scientific advances to be specifically described are those involving the application to human beings of the results of future research in biology, physiology and psychology. It is only by means of the science of life that the quality of life can be radically changed. The sciences of matter can be applied in such a way that they will destroy life or make the living of it complex and uncomfortable; but, unless used as instruments by the biologists and psychologists, they can do nothing to modify the natural forms and expressions of life itself. ... This really revolutionary revolution is to be achieved, not in the external world, but in the souls and flesh of human beings.

— Aldous Huxley, preface to the 1946 edition of *Brave New World*

Over the course of the past century, two modern dystopias captured the imagination of people more than any other literary works of their kind. Many read Aldous Huxley's *Brave New World* and George Orwell's *Nineteen Eighty-Four* as prophesies or admonitions that if humankind were not careful, the future might look like *this.* Of the two, Orwell's novel seemed to portray the more plausible future. It depicted a technologically advanced version of the sorts of totalitarian regimes with which the twentieth century was all too familiar. Today, because of recent extraordinary advances in biomedicine, biotechnology, and communications uncannily anticipated by Huxley, *Brave New World* seems more relevant. Yet in *Brave New World Revisited,* published in 1958, even Huxley doubted that the reproductive technology that made his imagined world so radically different from anything man had experienced in the past was likely to come very soon. "Babies in bottles and the centralized control of reproduction are not perhaps impossible," Huxley opined, "but it is quite clear that for a long time to come we shall remain a viviparous species breeding at random."

A half-century later, "babies in bottles" are not yet on the horizon, but "designer" genes and cloned babies are. Over the past fifty years, mankind has developed a dizzying array of biotechnologies (e.g., artificial insemination, in-vitro fertilization, and gene-splicing) that if fully implemented or mandated by government would leave increasingly less to chance in human reproduction. Thus, the imminent prospect of cloning a human, while it may be the most compelling sign of this revolution, is by no means the only one along the well-marked path towards the mastery of our genetic makeup. All of this has prompted a number of social critics to return with renewed interest to *Brave New World* as an admonitory tale.

Here, however, I am less interested in adding to recent speculations about the scientific and technological advances that could cause our society to resemble *Brave New World* than with some of the moral and theological questions the story raises about the wisdom of altering our own nature. In the passage excerpted above, from the preface to the 1946 edition of *Brave New World,* Huxley explains that his principal purpose was not to write a political novel about the external arrangements of a future society but rather to describe a revolution inside of human nature itself brought about mainly by the biological sciences. "The sciences of matter can be applied in such a way that they will destroy life or make the living of it complex and uncomfortable." Huxley writes, "but, unless used as instruments by the biologists and psychologists, they can do nothing to modify the natural forms and expressions of life itself.... *The really revolutionary revolution is to be achieved, not in the external world, but in the souls and flesh of human beings* [my emphasis].

Huxley did not write *Brave New World* as prophecy. It is instead an artful satire that follows in the great English tradition of Thomas More's *Utopia,* Jonathan Swift's *Gulliver's Travels,* and Alexander Pope's *Dunciad.* Huxley juxtaposes two vastly different future societies. The first, the so-called *Brave New World,* is a global order that claims to have rid the earth of suffering and perfected the universal human goal of happiness. Liberalism and democracy have been mercifully put to rest. In their place, a regime of social engineers keeps the people happy. These managers are *Brave New World's* version of Plato's philosopher-king. Consumption and entertainment conjoin the social mass, and a drug-induced religion of social solidarity supplies genial concord and fantasies of perpetual bliss. When one first enters the story, *Brave New World* seems to have little resemblance to contemporary society. But quickly it is evident that certain noteworthy characteristics and trends of contemporary life have taken strange and unexpected form in *Brave New World.* Like other great satirists, Huxley aims to demonstrate that what looks like normality to those immersed in the present may not be so. He wants to remind the reader of those cultural values and criteria of judgment that have historically preserved and enhanced that which is most noble in man. At bottom, Huxley is not only a satirist but, as satirists often are, a humanist as well.

In *Brave New World* the state employs advanced biological and behavioral sciences to manufacture and control its citizens. And this is certainly our major interest. But Huxley also holds up to scorn and ridicule many other aspects of the contemporary world to which modern people are attracted and in which they often invest a great deal of value, including consumerism, the commodification of the body, our forms of recreation and entertainment, and the cult of celebrity.

Even Huxley's tightly managed global civilization finds it necessary, however, to maintain sequestered "primitive" societies—Native American Reservations, such as the one in New Mexico where John, the principal protagonist of the story, was raised. The Reservation is a degraded throwback to "past" societies. In it, traditional religion and family relations persist, while love and hatred and freedom and violence play themselves out in familiar ways. In this dark and primitive society, the reader also sees significant elements of the modern world. While the Indians' sense of honor and adherence to strict rules of sexual conduct and religious practice may be admirable, their lives are marked also by brutality, abject poverty, and disease. Would one really want to live in such a place? John, who was raised on the Reservation but whose mother is from the "civilized" world, struggles with a kind of dual "citizenship." Where does he belong, on the Reservation or in civilization? Where does man belong, and what is his true nature? Huxley's strange tale evokes these questions.

Like More and Swift, Huxley takes us to "other worlds" that are sufficiently unlike ours that we allow ourselves to put down our guard. Yet they are also familiar enough that we cannot wholly disassociate ourselves from them. They are like the mirrors in an amusement park that by distorting and exaggerating our physical features cause us to look at ourselves in startling new ways. In these mirrors, we are led to see dark possibilities of the contemporary world, which, under ordinary circumstances, we do not perceive. By tampering, for example, with man's biological and sexual constitution to promote health and quality of life, we may be embarking on a course that, in C. S. Lewis's famous phrase, will bring about "the abolition of man." The controllers and managers of *Brave New World* have replaced sexual procreation with the standardized manufacture of human beings. By means of an advanced cloning technology, the individuals of *Brave New World* are genetically tailored to perform productive functions and exercise consumptive behaviors that make society a well-oiled machine. They have abolished marriage and the family to satisfy the human desire for individual autonomy, sexual freedom, and the unrestricted pursuit of entertainment and recreational pleasure. In the place of marriage and the family they have installed a total system of behavioral conditioning that renders the denizens of *Brave New World* ready to live lives in total loyalty to the state. They live by the motto, "Every one belongs to everyone else," yet have been constituted so as to be unfit to carry on a lasting relationship with any one person in particular.

Huxley thus highlights trends in contemporary society that he suspects may lead eventually to the erasure of some of the fundamental attributes of our humanity. Huxley was not a Christian believer. But the Christian tradition and Victorian legacy had shaped his moral imagination so that he believed, for example, that human sexuality is not reducible merely to an animal passion for pleasure and that sexual promiscuity abases human culture. He embraced, in his own secular fashion, the sacredness of human life and the dignity of the person. He understood that wisdom and moral truths, settled on for millennia in Western culture, were under assault. And that troubled him.

In *Brave New World*, Huxley does not defend unambiguously traditional religious and moral norms. But a writer of fiction is not obliged to do so. It is sufficient that he imaginatively brings these matters to his reader's attention and challenges him to weigh them seriously. One aim of the satirist is to rouse the reader to a recognition that the core beliefs and sentiments about human nature that he or she takes for granted are not self-evident to every one and might not persist under all conditions—for example, if the religious or philosophical traditions out of which they have arisen atrophy. Who can deny that some of the strongest sentiments concerning the value of individual human life held by modern persons, even non-religious ones, grew in the soil of the Christian religion? Is it not plausible that when that religion weakens, these sentiments may also dissipate, despite the efforts of some to ground them in philosophical reason or secular ethics? In *Brave New World*, no one gives a second thought to whether it is immoral, inappropriate, or distasteful to engineer the distinct genetic composition of each and every individual or to let the state decide when the time has come for a person to be euthanized for the good of society at large.

As I have said, *Brave New World* is not a political novel. It is, rather, a humanistic work. Huxley dares his reader to reconsider the nature of the sexual revolution and where it might be headed. He asks whether, through the biological sciences and psychology, modern man has already begun to disassemble himself. He cautions modern folk, who think or assume that they can continuously redefine or reconstruct primary forms of human relationship without risk, that their actions may lead to unintended, un-anticipated, and unwanted consequences. Early in the novel, Mustafa Mond, one of the World Controllers, addresses a group of students on tour at the Central London Hatchery and Conditioning Center.

> "Just try to realize it," he [Mustafa Mond] said, and his voice sent a strange thrill quivering along their diaphragms. "Try to realize what it was like to have a viviparous mother."
>
> That smutty word again. But none of them dreamed, this time, of smiling.
>
> "Try to imagine what 'living with one's family' meant."
> They tried, but obviously without the smallest success.
> "And do you know what a 'home' was?"
> They shook their heads....
> "Home, home—a few small rooms, stiflingly over-inhabited by a man, by a periodically teeming woman, by a rabble of boys and girls of all ages. No air, no space; an understerilized prison; darkness, disease, and smells.... Psychically, it was a rabbit hole, a midden, hot with the frictions of tightly packed life, reeking with emotion. What suffocating intimacies, what dangerous, insane, obscene relationships between the members of the family group! Maniacally, the mother brooded over her children ... like a cat over its kittens ... 'My baby, and oh, oh, at my breast, the little hands, the hunger, and that unspeakable agonizing pleasure! ...'"

"Yes," said Mustafa Mond, nodding his head, "you may well shudder."

. . . "The world was full of fathers—was therefore full of misery; full of mothers—therefore full of every kind of perversion from sadism to chastity; full of brothers, sisters, uncles, aunts—full of madness and suicide."

When I introduce *Brave New World* in the classroom, many students are troubled by this scene. It discomforts them. Their sentiments lean in the other direction. They do not know quite how to handle the repulsion of the inhabitants of *Brave New World* toward marriage, parenthood, and family. They have a difficult time translating their own deepest sentiments into moral arguments. Though they imagine that their views about God are relevant to their views about human nature and society, the theists in the classroom do not know how to make the connection. In these respects they are typically modern people. They strongly depend on sentiments that once had a sure foundation in biblical faith, but now are like the foam left on a beach after the receding of the tide. Most of my students are repulsed by the prospect of human cloning. Yet they are reduced to naked, emotive responses to Huxley's persuasive fictional presentation of people who are equally repulsed by monogamous marriage and biological motherhood. Huxley's insights into our age of sentiments and his ability to put this *zeitgeist* to a hard test constitute part of the genius of his novel.

My students do not lack familiarity with the bioethical issues and questions that the press routinely talks about or that countless textbooks rehearse. They are much less familiar, however, with the fundamental Christian dogmas of the Trinity, Incarnation, and Resurrection that ground the religious argument for the sacredness of human life. They are nearly as ill equipped to defend the case for chaste and monogamous marriage as the inhabitants of *Brave New World*. Huxley does not make it easy for them to avoid this difficult conclusion about themselves.

The Genesis story is reversed in Huxley's tale. In Genesis, the fullness and completeness of humankind is man-womanhood, not man alone or woman alone. From Adam is drawn Eve, no less a human being than himself. Nevertheless, the two are not whole or complete unless joined by conjugal love to form a one-flesh union. And from this love union they in turn bring another into being, the child who shares their flesh and, receiving their love, reciprocates it with his or her filial affection. As the late Protestant ethicist Paul Ramsey says in his prescient book *Fabricated Man* (1970): "We procreate new beings like ourselves in the midst of our love for one another, and in this there is a trace of the original mystery by which God created the world because of his love." This love union of the two, completed by a third, is the microcosm of human society and sociality and the very similitude of the Holy Trinity.

Huxley's novel is not inspired by a Christian worldview. It is not even especially sympathetic to Christianity. But Huxley is not uninterested in the religious question. He is conscious that more than ethical decision-making, however scrupulously conducted, is at issue. Freedom and morality have a social and historical context. A whole social world is at stake, and Christianity has played a formative role in that world's history.

This much can be said about Christian religion as a theme in the novel. The reader learns that the inhabitants of *Brave New World* deliberately have been kept ignorant of biblical faith and so are not able to articulate what the value of their lives is apart from strict standards of social utility. They have no knowledge of the bedrock belief upon which Western culture, with its respect for the transcendent worth of the individual, was founded. In their world, the worth of the individual is measured not by the character or law of God but by the individual's contribution to social stability and the general happiness of all. In a conversation with John, who has some knowledge of the Christian faith, Mustafa Mond proudly explains why Christianity is no longer needed. He responds to John's plea that for the sake of human dignity and mankind's struggle to be noble, the people of *Brave New World* should know about God. John exclaims: "If you allowed yourselves to think of God, you wouldn't allow yourselves to be degraded by pleasant vices. You'd have a reason for bearing things patiently, for doing things with courage. I've seen it with the Indians." Mond answers:

> "My dear young friend . . . civilization has absolutely no need of nobility or heroism. These things are symptoms of political inefficiency. In a properly organized society like ours, nobody has any opportunities for being noble or heroic. . . . The greatest care has been taken to prevent you from loving any one too much. There's no such thing as divided allegiance; you're so conditioned that you can't help doing what you ought to do. And what you ought to do is on the whole pleasant, so many of the natural impulses are allowed free play, that there really isn't any temptation to resist. And if ever, by some unlucky chance, anything unpleasant should somehow happen, why, there's always *soma* to give you a holiday from facts. Anybody can be virtuous now. You can carry at least half your morality about in a bottle. Christianity without tears—that's what *soma* is.

Seventy-five years ago, G. K. Chesterton wrote on similar themes. He described how modern man's loss of a transcendent image of himself is exposed by the debate over eugenics. In an article titled "The Fallacy of Eugenics," Chesterton observes:

> We breed cows for milk; and not for a moral balance of particular virtues in the cow. We breed pigs to turn them into pork, not to exhibit their portraits as pictures of perfect and harmonious beauty. In other words, we breed cows and pigs precisely because we cannot really criticize cows and pigs. We cannot judge them from the point of view of the Cow

Concept or the Pig Ideal. Therefore we cannot, and do not, criticize them in the way in which we criticize our fellow creatures (always provided, of course, that they are our poorer fellow-creatures) when we call them feeble-minded; or when we betray our own feeble-mindedness by calling them Unfit. For the very word Unfit reveals the weakness of the whole of this pseudo-scientific position. We should say that a cow is fit to provide us with milk; or that a pig is unfit to provide us with pork. But nobody would call up the insanely isolated vision of the Unfit Pig in the abstract. But when we talk about human beings, we are bound to break off the sentence in the middle; we are bound to call them Unfit in the abstract. For we know how varied, how complex, how controversial are the questions that arise about the functions for which they should be fitted.

In *Brave New World* and increasingly in our world, people take it for granted that we possess the biological, psychological, and sociological tools to measure whether or not this or that human life is fit to be born or fit to go on living. Some social scientists and contemporary ethicists even make lists of those physical and psychological capacities that they think an individual must possess for that individual to be regarded as person or for him to have a right to life.

A type of cloning commonly practiced today to reproduce desirable traits in livestock has been perfected in *Brave New World*. This is split-embryo cloning, which imitates the natural twinning process. Somatic cell nuclear transfer cloning, the process by which Dolly the sheep was made (Dolly, by the way, died because of premature aging), is not imagined. But however cloning is done, this moral consideration, posed by Huxley in his novel, inevitably arises: How are we learning to look at ourselves by practicing this form of procreation? At first glance cloning may not seem to entail an instrumental attitude towards human life and its value. Some would argue that cloning promises to be just one more reproductive technology that assists persons to have children who otherwise would not be able to have them, or to help couples ensure that their child is not afflicted by a disease of which they may be carriers. But when men and women forget that they are created in the image and likeness of God and that human personhood, freedom, and community have a divine prototype and origin, then cloning may gradually come to be viewed as a means by which to take up a Promethean project of reinventing ourselves according to just the sorts of instrumental criteria that C. S. Lewis describes.

At base, these instrumental criteria, applied to human procreation, fail because they ignore the principal reason why human beings desire to have children: *the need to love and be loved*. Modern folk tend to confuse the biblical belief about the *imago Dei* with the simple assertion that human life is of special value because human beings possess reason and the freedom to choose. Yet even the denizens of *Brave New World* may be described as rational and free to make their own decisions. Nonetheless, they are denatured and crippled human beings because they cannot love, perhaps ultimately because they were not conceived in love. They have been designed and conditioned not to love, and, more importantly, the elimination of marriage, sexual procreation, and parenthood has removed the "natural" conditions in which intimacy and attachment grow.

Love, not reason, is the defining and ennobling characteristic of our humanity. The less we love, the more we are denatured. The more we love, the deeper is the stamp of the image of God on our nature. Love is relational and is expressed quintessentially through sex, marriage, conjugal union, procreation, and the family. This love is not merely natural; it is divine. Science is unable to explain its mystery or to ensure through eugenics that people love one another. In the One Godhead, love unites God the Father, God the Son, and God the Holy Spirit in an indivisible union. This mutually reciprocated love of the Three Who are One brings into being Creation and, most especially, human beings whom God makes in his very own image in order to be loved and to love. Love draws man and woman together so that the child who is born to them is a sign, signature, and extension into the world of the love they share.

Early on in the cloning debate, the question was raised as to whether a clone would have a soul and whether it could or would be treated with the respect due a human person. This was a profoundly mistaken and misleading question. Biblical and Christian anthropology holds that the human being is a "living soul," an expression that the ancients used to identify the whole person, not just a spiritual substance. Every human being is by nature a psychosomatic unity, or a living soul. Biblical faith excludes the body-and-soul dualism that the question implies. If a living human being is physically present, then so, too, is a soul present, and vice-versa. I think the matter is fairly simple. By whatever means a human being is conceived, that human being is a living soul, whether he or she be conceived through sexual procreation or cloning. Human beings do not *possess* souls; they are *enfleshed* souls or *ensouled* bodies, whichever you please. Body and soul together constitute a human person in the full moral sense.

The really important question for a Christian responding to the prospect of cloning is not whether a cloned human being has a soul, but whether cloning respects the church's understanding of human nature and the meaning of human sexuality and love. This is not solely a subject of dogma and doctrine. It is raised by the performance of the Christian sacraments. For example, what are Christians affirming about a human being, even an infant, by baptizing him or her? What does the union of man and woman form when they are joined in Holy Matrimony? And why do Christians perform funeral and burial services for dead people? How are even dead people valuable to us? Why do Christians conscientiously remember the dead? To all of these questions the logic leads back to love.

In *Brave New World* the dead are forgotten. They are forgotten even before they die, as they are sent to hospitals where dying is not only done but accelerated. It is hospice "gone south," to use a contemporary colloquialism, where the last social service rendered unto the individual is euthanasia. The final value of the individual is a societal measurement according to the same utilitarian principle that produced his or her manu-facture. As one of the characters explains to a friend, "All men are psychochemically equal," just as all provide "indispensable services" to society. As "every one works for every one else," so at life's end every one gives back to society this same value by being cremated. "Phosphorous recovery," explained Henry telegraphically. "On their way up the chim-ney the gases go through four separate treatments. P_2O_5 used to go right out of circulation every time they cremated some one. Now they recover over ninety-eight per cent of it. More than a kilo and a half per corpse. . . . Fine to think we can go on being socially useful even after we're dead. Making plants grow."

The logic is undeniable in *Brave New World*. Because human beings are manufactured for their genetic makeup so as to insure that society runs smoothly, pleasantly, and efficiently, the sum of the pleasure and productivity the individual puts into society constitutes his or her "hu-man" value. In *Brave New World*, the unconditionality of love endangers society because it has no immediate social utility, just as the lover's affir-mation of the immeasurable worth of the beloved is necessarily antisocial since the standard of value is personal and not societal. Are we headed into the same sort of world by our embrace of reproductive technologies that teach us to value our offspring for the genetic makeup we chose for them?

In *Brave New World*, our humanity has not only been debiologized but also despiritualized. This entails the abolition of parenthood and it pre-vents the deep and profound love commitment of husband and wife that spreads mysteriously into the world through the issuance of their fleshly union. *Brave New World* is a world without love, and so it also is a desper-ately lonely place. That loneliness cuts to the core of every citizen and is momentarily relieved but not remedied by *soma*, the feelie movies, and the orgiastic religion of the Solidarity Service. In *Fabricated Man*, Paul Ramsey cites an article titled "The Second Genesis" that the science fic-tion writer Albert Rosenfeld published in the June 1969 issue of *Life* magazine. Rosenfeld warns of the unbearable loneliness that full employment of our new reproductive technologies may bring about and the harm that this will do to our *humanum*, our humanity.

> In our current circumstances, the absence of a loved one saddens us, and death brings terrible grief. Think how easily the tears could be wiped away if there were no single "loved one" to miss that much—or if that loved one were readily replaceable by any of several others.
>
> And yet—if you (the hypothetical *in vitro* man) did not miss anyone very much, neither would anyone miss *you* very much. Your absence would cause little sadness, your death little grief. You too would be readily replaceable....
>
> The aloneness many of us feel on this earth is assuaged, more or less effectively, by the relationships we have with other human beings.... These relationships are not always as deep or as abiding as we would like them to be.... Yet... there is always the hope that each man and woman who has not found such relationships will eventually find them. But in the *in vitro* world, or the tissue-culture world, even the hope of deep, abiding relationships might be hard to sustain. Could society devise adequate substitutes? If each of us is "forever a stranger and alone" here and now, how much more strange, how much more alone, would we feel in a world where we belong to no one and no one belongs to us. Could the trans-humans of post-civilization survive without love as we have known it in the institutions of marriage and family?

Let us be frank and admit that in our divorce and consumer culture some of this has already come to pass. We are raising many children who at an early age must ask themselves, "To whom do I matter?" "To whom do I belong?" And when these persons become adults they may be less

174

likely than others to form strong human attachments. They may even fear such attachments. One wishes that this experience would leave us that much more wary of accelerating the pace at which we are producing separation, alienation, aloneness, and fragile human ties. But we are doing just the opposite, which may leave us even more willing to accept the disassembly and reconstruction of our humanity from the inside out as the normal, even inevitable price of progress. Huxley's novel is now more than seventy years old. Yet its message is as fresh as the day it was written, and its admonition that man is in jeopardy of abolishing his humanity through the misuse of his own highest scientific achievement even more timely.

13

Why Should Businessmen Read Great Literature?

Reading maketh a full man; conference a ready man; and writing an exact man.

— Sir Francis Bacon

Leisure without human letters amounts to death, the entombment of a living man.

— Saint William Fermat

Nothing makes a man more reverent than a library.

— Sir Winston Churchill

*I*n every society, power must be humanized and used morally in order that free and civilized life might prosper. And in a commercial society, businessmen and businesswomen wield especially great power and are frequently called into roles of civic and political leadership. This fact makes the question that serves as this chapter's title especially significant. A half-century ago, Russell Kirk, author of *The Conservative Mind,* penned an article titled "The Inhumane Businessman." Kirk did not argue that businessmen are, as a lot, more inhumane, mean, or cruel than the average bank clerk, schoolteacher, or construction worker. But he was persuaded that businessmen are "deficient in the disciplines which nurture sound imagination and strong moral character," and that this does not augur well for the nation.

Kirk lamented the turn to business education in our colleges and universities, which, he argued, contributes to the cultural illiteracy of the business class. This trend toward specialized business education accelerated during the concluding decades of the twentieth century, leaving fewer and fewer of those engaged in business educated in the liberal arts. That is a principal reason why businessmen so often do not read great literature. So this is where I shall begin.

Imagining larger possibilities and purposes

Kirk was right. By the 1950s, higher education in North America had begun to buy into business education, so to speak, and replace liberal arts studies with this glamorized version of vocational training. Colleges certainly did not heed C. S. Lewis's admonition that "if education is beaten by training, civilization dies." Even earlier in the century, G. K. Chesterton published an article in the *London Illustrated Times,* titled simply enough "On Business Education," in which, in his acerbic manner, he summed up the scandal and hinted at its consequences: "Modern educators begin by stuffing the child, not with the sense of justice by which he can judge the world, but with the sense of inevitable doom or dedication by which he must accept that particular very worldly aspect of the world."

I teach core curriculum courses in ethics, literature, and theology at a college in which more than a third of the students are business majors. And I have seen over the past twenty years how business "training" sucks these students dry of idealism and replaces it with the crudest forms of pragmatism, utilitarianism, and fatalism. The light in their eyes has already begun to dim and flicker before they have finished their fourth year, a dreadful thing to witness. Despite my efforts and those of other teachers in the humanities, many men and women depart Loyola College with no sense of the meaning or value of a liberal arts education. Nor have they acquired the habits of reading that are historically associated with such an education.

This deficiency is debilitating in ways that are wholly overlooked by much of society, including the parents of my students. For if these young men and women learned the meaning and value of the liberal arts, they would leave college with the answers to two questions that, as it turns out, they hardly know how to ask, let alone answer. First, "Why should I read great literature throughout the rest of my life?" Second, "Why am I choosing to spend my life in business?"

They cannot answer the second question satisfactorily because they were not encouraged in college (or even permitted, in many cases) to read and love the great literary masters. Aristotle, Dante, Shakespeare, Dostoevsky, and Eliot teach us to imagine larger possibilities and purposes for our lives. They test our decisions with the moral wisdom of humankind. They ask us to move through the world with discernment. They show us that we possess the freedom to make of our lives what we will and not what others choose for us, what the fates decide, or what historical forces dictate.

Robert Louis Stevenson's essay "On the Choice of a Profession" gets to the crux of these concerns. The essay is composed in the form of a letter to a young man who is seeking advice on a career. It has a sharp satirical edge worthy of Pope or Swift. At one point, Stevenson introduces an imaginary conversation with a banker friend.

> "My good fellow," I say, "give me a moment."
> "I have not a moment to spare," says he.
> "Why?" I enquire.
> "I must be banking," he replies. . . .
> "And what," I continue my interrogatory, "is banking?"
> "Sir," says he, "it is my business."
> "Your business?" I repeat. "And what is a man's business?"

"Why," cries the banker, "a man's business is his duty."

Stevenson then offers these observations about the conversation:

> But this is a sort of answer that provokes reflection. Is a man's
> business his duty? Or perhaps should not his duty be his
> business? If it is not my duty to conduct a bank (and I contend
> that it is not) is it the duty of my friend the banker? Who told
> him it was? Is it in the Bible? Is he sure that banks are a good
> thing? Might it not be his duty to stand aside and let some
> one else conduct the bank? Or perhaps ought he not to have
> been a ship-captain instead? All these perplexing queries may
> be summed up under one head: the grave problem which my
> friend offers to the world: Why is he a Banker?

The loss of leisure and the dragon of despair

Through the back door, Stevenson has introduced the ancient tradition of
the man of virtuous character. This tradition says that the virtues are not
the same as the skills needed to perform work—and furthermore, that
duty, which is most certainly related to the virtues, carries moral weight.
Duty is related to conscience and a higher law. To say that "business is my
duty" ignores this fact and reveals ignorance of what duty and virtue really are. That is why Stevenson quips: "Who told him it was [his duty]? Is
it in the Bible?" Of course the Bible did not instruct his friend (nor does it
instruct anyone else) that it was his duty to be a banker. Banking may be a
man's choice of work, but duty impinges upon work as the transcendent
obligation to do what is morally right in every location or vocation.

Duty is the "business" of being a virtuous human being. Doing business is not a duty, although it may be one's duty to behave virtuously in

business. That is why Stevenson wonders: "Is he sure that banks are a good thing?" For it can never be one's duty to do evil. A contractual agreement or a compelling love for making financial transactions may persuade a person to be a banker, but it may be a person's duty to foreswear an unscrupulous bank dealing or even to leave one's position in the bank altogether. Nothing in Stevenson's friend's statements suggests that he has thought through these matters or that he even knows how to begin to evaluate his position morally. He is a man with a shrunken moral imagination, though we do not know how precisely he got that way.

Finally, Stevenson's friend does not even know why he is a banker. The main reason, Stevenson speculates, is that he "was trapped" by a form of education that "harnesses a fellow" with the best of intentions but makes him a slave before he has had a chance to become a free man. The fellow was kept in the shadows of Plato's cave—kept in the dark, as we say. He chose to become a banker because, presumably, he could not imagine doing any other work. He had been fed innumerable facts about how to conduct the business of banking but was not challenged to ask the "why" questions about how to conduct his life. Stevenson continues:

> The fellow was hardly in trousers before they whipped him into school; hardly done with school before they smuggled him into an office . . . and all this before he has had time so much as to imagine that there may be any other practical course. Drum, drum, drum. . . . The trick is performed . . . ; the wild ass's colt is broken in; and now sits diligently scribbling. Thus it is, that out of men, we make bankers.

I do not know much about the banker of Stevenson's time. But I am familiar with today's counterpart. I have seen them already "broken in" in college. I have seen them riding the East Coast Metroliner, where I have watched young men and women who not only exhibit all the signs of not knowing the difference between duty and work, but also of not knowing how to leave work behind for genuine leisure. Not that these well-dressed men and women do not change into sports clothes and take vacations. They pursue recreation with a vengeance and make sure to dress in the best recreational attire. They work hard at taking a "break" from work, at getting good R&R, so that they are ready to go back to work. This is a state of mind that never *leaves* work. These businessmen and business-women, young and old, are overcome by what the philosopher Josef Pieper has called *acedia,* a form of lethargy not to be confused with idleness. (*Acedia,* you will remember, is another name for sloth, traditionally reckoned among the seven capital sins.) At the bottom of *acedia's* pit is the dragon of anxiousness and despair that renders its captives unable to be alone with themselves. In other words, the lethargy of *acedia* is a loss of the capacity to be with oneself and to live reflectively rather than reflexively. Ironically, this incapacitation is manifested as unceasing restlessness and a flight from freedom and the self to business and work.

One need not follow these businessmen and businesswomen to their beach vacations at the Hamptons or their ski weekends in the Poconos to reach this diagnosis. Watch them in their extra-roomy Metroliner seats with no work to do and no one to be with but themselves. Instead of embracing this freedom as true leisure or an opportunity to read a good book, they turn on their cell phones and feverishly punch up anyone they might have the slightest excuse to call.

I have often been tempted to call across the aisle, "Good fellow" (or "Hey guy," to be up to date), "think of the wonderful tales that have been told and will be told, which you will never know. Read Eliot and Auden, Henry James and Graham Greene. They will help you get a grip on the life that is being sapped from you minute by minute by the dragon. I am sorry my colleagues did not assign such authors to you in college or inspire a love for them so that you would return to them often. And I am sorry that they never cultivated within you those habits of reading and reflection that make a person a free and full human being."

The only amateur animal

In a masterful defense of liberal learning titled "Our English Syllabus," C. S. Lewis emphasized that we are distinguished from the rest of God's creatures not by our capacity for work—all animals are workers and professionals at what they do—but by the fact that we alone may be amateurs in an infinite variety of activities at our leisure. He writes:

> You have noticed, I hope, that man is the only amateur animal; all the others are professionals. They have no leisure and do not desire it. When the cow has finished eating she chews the cud; when she has finished chewing she sleeps; when she has finished sleeping she eats again. She is a machine for turning grass into calves and milk—in other words, for producing more cows. The lion cannot stop hunting, nor the beaver building dams, nor the bee making honey. When God made the beasts dumb he saved the world from infinite boredom, for if they could speak they would all of them, all day, talk nothing but shop.

Yet I have seen that business education treats young men and women precisely as if they were destined to be at shop and to talk shop all day long. Even the liberal arts have been influenced by this slavish and utilitarian view of human nature. We prepare young people to become cows and mules rather than men and women. We expend great energy and dedicate vast sums of money towards directing all of youth's energy into the pursuit of a career. We are more concerned that our students learn to be professionals and prepare themselves for careers than we are that they learn about the human condition and cultivate the moral imagination. My guild has sent out into society far too many souls whose imaginations are starved, who do not know what to do with themselves when they are not at work other than to feed appetites that will never be satisfied and to pursue pleasures that will never bring happiness.

Recently, one young fellow, a senior who had "escaped the business school," as he put it, in order to pursue a political science major, came to my office to tell me that many of his friends who were graduating as business majors were gloomy and listless because they were leaving Loyola College without jobs. Most had become business majors solely because they were told that they *would* have a job when it was all over. Few really enjoyed their studies. "Now they haven't the foggiest notion of why they spent four years of their lives in college or what to do with themselves after graduation," he said. "It's grim, really depressing, to be around them."

But it is never too late to become a free man, to become "a full man," as Bacon said, by reading the masters. Read them, and the desire for perfection will take hold of you, love and not lust will rule your life, confidence in living today and not anxiety for finishing tomorrow's work will punctuate your every day, and you will attract good company.

One evening, my son, then a year out of college, got together with three of his high school classmates, another young man and two young women, at a singles' establishment in Baltimore. My son works in the brave new world of computer technologies, in which he does technical tasks, teaches, and writes for computer gaming magazines. I did not ask what kind of work his friends are doing. But all of them majored in English, so that when this opportunity arrived to spend some leisure time together, all four brought something to share and talk about other than shop or the season finale of *Friends* or *Sex and the City*. They talked about the great authors whom in college they read and learned to love—especially Charles Dickens. This real-life scene, more real than any reality TV show, is a microcosm of the birth and rebirth of genuine culture. This is where leisure lends meaning to all the rest of one's life, including work. This is as it should be for that one creature that God made to be an amateur (Latin: *amare, amator*) rather than a professional. We are created to be principally lovers, not laborers.

We have come full circle. Why should businessmen and businesswomen read the classics? The answer is simple: to be free, and in that freedom to grow into fuller, more complete, more virtuous, and more interesting human beings who share with each other a living and life-giving culture. If Stevenson's imaginary banker had understood this, he would not have called business his duty and would have been able to give a quite sufficient explanation as to why he was a banker.

Vital moral maps of this world

Great literature, whether it is history, biography, humane letters, poetry, or fiction, "cannot substitute for native shrewdness and familiarity with worldly wisdom, but it can supplement and elevate such worldly wisdom," says Russell Kirk, wisely. Great literature has the power to ennoble our lives by helping us to put ourselves in the other's shoes. It teaches us much about the hopes and motivations of our fellow human beings that our everyday experience may not provide. And it draws for us vital moral maps of this world with its exemplary stories of evil and good character tested and forged in the furnace of the human comedy. The result ought to be "the cultivation," as Kirk says, "of tastes ... [and] disciplines ... that enable the pleasures of humane consciousness to make their way naturally and gracefully into even the busiest career." In his estimate and also mine, this should lead not only to greater longevity, but, more importantly, to a life better lived.

What to read?

"If we take literature in the widest sense, so as to include the literature of both knowledge and power, the question 'What is the good of reading what anyone writes?' is very like the question 'What is the good of listening to what anyone says?,'" writes C. S. Lewis. "Unless you contain in yourself sources that can supply all the information, entertainment, advice, rebuke, and merriment you want, the answer is obvious." There are myriad such sources. Here are just a few.

Working: Its Meaning and Its Limits is an excellent and eclectic anthology of brief readings edited by Gilbert Meilaender. Witold Rybczynski's *Waiting for the Weekend* tracks leisure's historical development and transformation by modern commercial culture. *Leisure: The Basis of Culture* by Josef Pieper is a recognized classic, presenting an apologia for the practice of contemplation in the midst of activity.

So-called leadership studies is a popular genre, but it is better to read actual stories about real leaders. Martin Gilbert's *Churchill: A Life* is the best one-volume biography of one of the greatest leaders of the twentieth century; Lord Charnwood's *Abraham Lincoln: A Biography* is the best of the greatest nineteenth-century leader; and David McCullough's *John Adams* is the best biography of one of the eighteenth century's most impressive men.

"To ask and then to answer these questions as far as one can, one needs above all a priceless and taxing involvement with truth and beauty," the novelist Mark Helprin writes. "Nowhere do they run together with such complexity and power as in the gracefully written word." Some novels of particular interest to those engaged in the active life include Walker Percy's *Moviegoer,* William Faulkner's *Absalom, Absalom,* William Shakespeare's *Tempest,* Leo Tolstoy's *Anna Karenina,* Joseph Conrad's *Heart of Darkness,* and Fyodor Dostoevsky's *Brothers Karamozov.* There are, of course, many others; *Invitation to the Classics,* edited by Louise Cowan and Os Guinness, provides one indispensable reading list that would take a lifetime to complete.

· *4* ·

Politics
and
Freedom

14

The Narrative of Freedom

The week after the terrorist attacks of September 11, 2001, President George W. Bush addressed a joint session of Congress. He gave in many respects an eloquent and well-crafted speech. It set down with considerable skill the meaning of the attacks and reasons to launch the war on terrorism. Nonetheless, the President made few references to America's national experience that might have supplied images and metaphors to help Americans draw instructive analogies to contemporary events and give concrete meaning to his apologia for freedom.

I want to explore the importance of rhetoric in keeping alive a nation's collective memory. For a society to have a sense of its purpose in history, rhetoric is necessary. Great political rhetoric moves the individual and the nation by evoking an ideal or supreme image of who they are as a people and how they fit into the greater scheme of things, how they relate to God or destiny. But to make such an image palpable, the rhetorician must attend to the chain of lesser images that rises to that supreme image.

Sensationalist freedom

It was most appropriate for the president to put freedom at the center of his speech. But it was also necessary for him to set out significant benchmarks in the history of that freedom, benchmarks that define and vindicate it. Abraham Lincoln employed this method almost perfectly in the Gettysburg Address. There Lincoln set forth the Union as his central governing image and led his listeners, through a tight chain of allusions to the origin and history of the United States, to a fuller sense of its meaning and the war being fought for it.

Freedom is not "just another word for nothin' left to lose," as Janice Joplin famously sang. Nor is freedom the liberty of the individual to do whatever pleases him so long as no one gets hurt, as so many of my college students honestly believe. But many, many Americans embrace this highly privatized and hedonistic notion of freedom.

The president did not have this sort of freedom in mind. Real political freedom is the felicitous condition under which justice may be purposively pursued. This political freedom has a narrative. It belongs to a history that needs to be told in order to inspire and ennoble those who possess it and are called to protect it. Great statesmen paint the past with the silver patina of myth, memory, and the moral imagination in order to elevate the minds of the people and move the national community to united action. But the president did not rehearse that narrative or tell that history. He did not take his listeners back to the founding and lead them through a chain of images of freedom embattled and freedom vindicated that would focus the mind's eye on the present moment of challenge.

The president was not the only one to miss this opportunity; the media did far worse. It did not seem to have occurred to any of the major television networks, for example, to lead their viewers through a reflection on the nation's extensive history of international engagement in order to help them make discerning judgments about the so-called war on terrorism. The media instead embraced sensationalism at almost every turn. They pandered to the passion for immediacy that so characterizes the modern temperament.

Those who are in special positions of influence within a society, whether they are parents or politicians, clergy, teachers, or the press, are obligated to exercise that society's collective memory to ensure that its tradition of freedom is handed on and renewed. Yet as a college professor I can say confidently and with great sadness that the young men and women in my classrooms are the most historically illiterate and politically uninformed that I have seen in more than twenty-five years of teaching. The fault does not rest solely on their teachers. It rests at least as much on parents, pastors, and civic leaders. All have allowed the rising generation to become captive to a popular culture that is self-centered, hedonistic, dangerously utilitarian, increasingly antagonistic to memory, and impious toward the past.

The exposed underbelly

This state of affairs has moved me to return of late to the work of Richard M. Weaver, an author whose writings made a strong impression on me in my formative years. The title of Weaver's best-known work now belongs to our popular vocabulary, even if most people familiar with the term "ideas have consequences" have not read his book. *Ideas Have Consequences* was published in 1948, more than a half-century ago. Yet it, along with others of Weaver's writings, speaks with startling insight to our present situation.

In the introduction, Weaver apologizes for offering the public yet "another book about the dissolution of the West." But *Ideas Have Consequences* is not *just* another book of that kind. Although Weaver undoubtedly had some books from the genre in mind—such as Oswald Spengler's *Decline of the West* and José Ortega y Gasset's *Revolt of the Masses*—his is unique in its attention to imagery and language as indicators of the spiritual and moral condition of a society. Weaver in his role as a teacher of rhetoric was a profound humanist and transcendental moralist.

On September 11, the new barbarians executed a great assault on the American social body. Their attack brought out great heroism, but it also exposed America's soft underbelly. For some time after that day the "Great Stereopticon"—Weaver's term for television, radio, and the printed media, the machinery of mass communication—spread throughout the land its images of our changed world. Daily—nay, hourly and minute by minute, interrupting itself with crawling headlines underneath the talking heads—it served up its own strange pictures of reality, images that were as debilitating as they were ubiquitous.

The magnitude, complexity, and reach of mass communication have increased vastly since Weaver's day, but he describes the character and nature of the Great Stereopticon with exceptional insight and foresight. The Stereopticon, he says, projects a highly selective and often nightmarish vision of the world, one composed largely of images of psychopathology, strife, and deadly force. Its malevolent gods bear down on us relentlessly and mercilessly. These are not so much images of what is "real" as they are the symptoms of cultural degradation. Writing even before the full impact of television, Weaver observes:

> The operators of the Stereopticon by their very selection of matter make horrifying assumptions about reality. For its audience that overarching dome becomes a sort of miasmic cloud, a breeder of strife and degradation and of the subhuman. What person taking the affirmative view of life can deny that the world served up daily by the press, movies, and radio is a world of evil and negation? There is iron in our nature sufficient to withstand any fact that is presented in a context of affirmation, but we cannot remain unaffected by the continued assertion of cynicism and brutality. Yet these are what the materialists in control of publicity give us.

Society, Weaver says, is not well served by images of wickedness and human degradation that are neither interpreted through historical memory nor transfigured by religious and moral imagination into a positive belief in the greater strength of goodness. "How common is it," he writes, "to see upon the front page of some organ destined for a hundred thousand homes the agonized face of a child run over in the street, the dying expression of a woman crushed by a subway train, tableaux of execution, scenes of intense grief. . . . The rise of sensational journalism everywhere testifies to man's loss of points of reference, to his determination to enjoy the forbidden in the name of freedom" while avoiding judgment and losing faith in a greater benevolence.

"Man is in the world to suffer his passion," Weaver continues. But the genuine creators and conservers of culture draw up images of man and society that resist "that 'sinking in upon the moral being'" of raw experience and emotion that is the death of a meaningful world. The genius and wisdom of the great poets and novelists, whether we are speaking of Dante, Dickens, and Dostoevsky, or Austen, Eliot, and Faulkner, is that, even as they expose vividly the character of evil, human suffering, and deadly untruth, they also show us how goodness, beauty, and truth shine light on a world that would otherwise slip into utter darkness.

No matter its boasts or pretensions, a civilization that is stripped of memory and the moral imagination is in jeopardy of collapsing in upon itself, its public world imploding into fragments of private desire and gratuitous brutality. The so-called realistic images that the Great Stereopticon projects onto the screen of the common life do not fortify belief. They may evoke pity for the other and pity for oneself, but they are incapable of leading us to a clear understanding of justice. They may stir the passions, but they do not strengthen the virtues.

The unifying vision

Weaver opens his chapter "The Great Stereopticon" with a passage that is reminiscent of what the philosopher Alasdair MacIntyre writes in his influential book *After Virtue*. MacIntyre argues that our society lacks a unifying vision of life and that this makes it difficult to sustain a coherent and truly just and beautiful public world. Shards of once whole religious and philosophical traditions litter the cultural landscape and are gathered up by individuals and groups who fling them at one another in bitter contests that have no real hope of resolution.

Like MacIntyre, Weaver judged that Western culture had lost the central metaphysical self-image that gave it purpose and a moral compass. Its inhabitants had sunk into emotivism, narcissism, and a desiccating individualism. Morality had become wholly subjective and the virtues, once the mortar of the social order, had morphed into undisciplined, competing passions.

MacIntyre says we are entering another dark age. Thirty years earlier, Weaver reached a similar conclusion:

> The darkling plain, swept by alarms, which threatens to be the world of our future, is an arena in which conflicting ideas, numerous after the accumulation of centuries, are freed from [the] discipline earlier imposed by ultimate conceptions. The decline is to confusion; we are agitated by sensation and look with wonder upon the serene somnambulistic creations of souls which had metaphysical anchorage. Our ideas become convenient perceptions, and we accept contradiction because we no longer feel the necessity of relating thoughts to the metaphysical dream.

He continues:

The problem which [this] disintegration places in the lap of practical men, those in charge of states, of institutions, of businesses, is how to persuade to communal activity people who no longer have the same ideas about the most fundamental things. In an age of shared belief, this problem does not exist, or there is a wide area of basic agreement. . . . The entire group is conscious of the tendency, which furnishes standards for value judgments. When the goal of life becomes self-realization, however, this vanishes. It vanishes right at that point where the ego asserts its independence; thereafter what reconciliation can there be between authority and the individual will? The politicians and businessmen are not interested in saving souls, but they are interested in preserving a minimum of organization, for upon that depend their posts and their incomes.

Weaver tried to show that *great* statesmen are concerned with more than mere survival. They strive even at the darkest moments of human history, like Churchill during the bombing of London, to persuade the people that there are truths worth fighting for, suffering for, and even dying for. Weaver claimed that civilized life depends on responsible public rhetoric. Rhetoric, not historical science, is what keeps alive a community's memory and infuses the common life with moral purpose.

Genuine rhetoric is more than the recitation of "facts." The modern press briefing sets the terms by which public policy may be debated and decided. But it is not truly rhetoric. True rhetoric moves beyond linear logic and the reporting of facts. It adopts analogical and figurative speech in order to probe the quiddity of things and their moral meaning. Neither is true rhetoric the mere excitation of human emotions through words or images. The Great Stereopticon floods us with words and images that excite the emotions and stimulate the appetites, but these words and images do little to enliven the moral imagination.

The sense of history

Neither the press briefing nor news programming, the dominant forms of "public speech" in our day, cultivate a sense of history. Neither strengthens or refines memory. Both instead breed what Richard Weaver called "presentism." "Presentism," he writes in his posthumously published book *Visions of Order*, "is the belief that only existence in the present can give significance to the thing." Yet living wholly in the present is not only impossible, but insofar as we seek to live in this manner, we rob ourselves of our humanity. Weaver argues that to the degree that people act without "memory and the extrapolation which it makes possible,"—that is, the use of analogy and the interpretation of meaning—"man becomes a kind of waif." Modern men and women who lack a sense of place and continuity with the past are driven by ephemeral appetites and the passion for immediate self-gratification.

The true rhetorician employs memory to show how even terrifying events like those of September 11 can be charged with redemptive meaning. He strives to demonstrate that we live in continuity with those who have gone before us, who also knew suffering, and that therefore there is reason to have courage and hope even when things seem at their worst. This is what Augustine did in *The City of God* to give courage and hope to Christians after the sack of Rome. And this is what is needed today from the president and other public leaders.

Richard Weaver taught that the forgetfulness of history lies behind the peculiarly modern impiety that inters with indifference the memory and wisdom of those who came before. It is also the mother of that enormous hubris that moves modern people to try to "create a new world out of [sheer] good will and ignorance." Today's true rhetorician would call you and me to a deep reformation of spirit, starting with a retrieval of all that we have sought to forget.

In the post–September 11 world, there is something haunting and prophetic about the closing words of *Ideas Have Consequences*.

Perhaps we shall have to learn the truth along some *via dolorosa*. It may be that we are awaiting a great change, that the sins of the fathers are going to be visited upon the generations until the reality of evil is again brought home and there comes some passionate reaction, like that which flowered in the chivalry and spirituality of the Middle Ages. If such is the most we can hope for, something toward that revival may be prepared by acts of thought and volition in this waning day of the West.

Postscript

On January 19, 2005, President George W. Bush delivered his second inaugural address to Congress, three years and three months after his speech on the horrific events of September 11, 2001. Most commentators did not rank the address among Bush's best, though it was "on message" and had rhetorical force, and few paid much regard to whether the president had endeavored to ground his apologetic for freedom and democracy in historical memory. By in large, he did not. Instead, the president issued a paean for freedom and democracy that rests in two abstract and dubious premises. The first is that because all humankind desires freedom, the course of world history is on freedom's side. The second is that democracy is freedom's measure. Where there is democracy, there is freedom. Where democracy is missing, there is only tyranny.

Some observers described Bush's rhetoric pejoratively as neo-Wilsonian. They faulted him for naïveté and excessive optimism about the inevitability of democracy. Others criticized him for speaking arrogantly and presumptuously about America's role in the global project of spreading freedom.

To be fair, the president took pains to say that Americans do not—and one presumes he meant, should not—regard themselves as especially

197

chosen by God to advance freedom and democracy wherever they see the need for it. He did, however, proclaim, "It is the policy of the United States to seek and support the growth of democratic movements and institutions in every nation and culture, with the ultimate goal of ending tyranny in our world." It is difficult not to interpret such speech as articulating not just policy but a mission.

The democratic elections that were to be held in Iraq a week after the inauguration served as the immediate backdrop for the president's speech. I can be counted as someone who does not believe that a democracy which in any strong sense resembles what Americans have known in the past or live under in the present will arise in Iraq. The analogies that pundits have made between the American founding and the processes in motion in Iraq are utterly misleading, not worthy of serious consideration. None of this means, however, that I believe the Iraqi people are doomed to continue to live under tyranny. But how Iraqis define and measure freedom in their own lives, in their own place, may well be different than our own definition and measure. I suspect the president was alluding to this when he stated that in Iraq "the institutions that arise may reflect customs and traditions very different from our own."

Nonetheless, Bush's inaugural was steeped in ideology, which by its nature is wedded to abstraction and averse to historical-mindedness. Ideology, of whatever sort, is constituted by two chief characteristics. First, it narrows the scope of our vision and understanding of the world, which politically can lead to serious missteps. Marxism, for example, claims that economics and the forces of production determine what the ruling class thinks and does. Human beings are fundamentally economic animals. Freedom is itself entirely a function of the economic system. Communism, which will destroy class structures, will thus bring into being true and absolute freedom. Ironically, libertarians, who embrace the free market as the ideal model of human commerce and exchange and are opposed to socialism of any kind, are also ideologues. They, too, view human beings narrowly as basically economic animals, but it is an individualistic and competitive economy that libertarians associate with ideal freedom. Second, ideology sets up a false absolute, almost a religion. Much was said in the twentieth century about the "religious" character of Marxist-Leninism, especially its utopian belief that world communism would usher in a new era of human freedom and perpetual peace.

In his second inaugural, George W. Bush offered a false, and ideological, philosophy of freedom. Let it be called *democratism*. Democratism makes popular plebiscite the standard of freedom. It virtually equates the *vox populi* with God's will. And it expresses a faith in the progress of democracy and freedom that imitates biblical notions of divine providence. "There is only one force of history," the president declared, "that can break the reign of hatred and resentment, and expose the pretensions of tyrants, and reward the hopes of the decent and tolerant, and that is the force of freedom." Democratism is the "religion" that preaches the global spread of freedom through the adoption of democratic political mechanisms, and this freedom is supposed to bring universal peace to all humankind. Whereas in his joint speech to Congress the president failed to render a discrete narrative of American freedom, in his inaugural he left his listeners to infer, since he told no such story, that there *is* a narrative of universal human freedom.

There isn't a global narrative of freedom, however. To suggest that there is and, correlatively, to make the abstract claim that there is an unqualified—unqualified by either human sin or history—universal human desire for freedom, is a serious error at best and a false religion at worst. To use this ideology to justify the use of American power is to dance dangerously with demons. For, as with all ideologies, it will be (consciously or unconsciously) used to disguise other motives, both good and bad.

Several days after Bush's inaugural address, the *Washington Post* ran an essay by the columnist David Ignatius titled "Reality Check for the Neo-Wilsonians." Ignatius told of a conversation that he had had with Mikheil Saakashvili, the newly elected and Western-oriented president of Georgia. While Saakashvili was grateful for the United States' support, he also pointed out that it "wasn't American power but a network of local and international institutions and partnerships," and the evolution of Georgian society, that gave his nation a chance of attaining true political freedom.

Even more telling is Saakashvili's story of a meeting with George W. Bush at the White House. The Georgian president "tried to engage Bush by telling him of Georgia's strategic importance because of its proximity to Caspian Sea oil. The president didn't seem interested [Saakashvili said]. It was only when Saakashvili began talking about freedom and liberty . . . that Bush got excited."

This story, unfortunately, testifies to the ideological framework of Bush's recent public speech. From Saakashvili, Bush was looking for information that would support his rhetoric and that might be assimilated into his project of spreading democracy throughout the world. He apparently did not see that a knowledge of Georgia's historical role in the region of the Caucasus is far more important in the practical political sense of lending support to Georgia's democratic aspirations than are platitudes about freedom's march.

There is no global narrative of freedom. But there certainly is an alternative to the ideology of democratism. It is a prudential politics that respects freedom but seriously takes into account the pluralism of human culture and the discrete histories of nations. The late Robert Nisbet, in his immensely important book *The Quest for Community,* published in 1953, wrote with sagacity that the idea of "popular sovereignty is not enough," nor is a simple faith in one man one vote, to insure genuine political freedom. "Because of our single-minded concentration upon the individual as the sole unit of society and upon the state as the sole source of legitimate power," argued Nisbet, "we have tended to overlook the fact that freedom thrives in cultural diversity, in local and regional differentiation, in associative pluralism, and above all, in the *diversification of power.*" One wishes that George W. Bush had reflected more on this sort of political wisdom in his second inaugural address. And one hopes that in the future the noble cause of human liberty is supported by such wisdom.

15

Nationalism,

A Non-Liberal Assessment

Early in the summer of 1990, I visited Armenia for the first time. My arrival was on the heels of the massive protests and rallies of 1987–88 and the terrible earthquake of December 1988. In Armenia, the conviction and expectation had spread that Gorbachev would fall from power—as indeed he did, fifteen months later—and talk everywhere was of independence. From a century filled with great tragedies for the Armenian people a nation would be born. Even the cautious and conservative Armenian Orthodox Church had begun to shift its position and support the popular nationalist movement.

How could I help but embrace these Armenian aspirations for sovereignty and self-determination? It looked as if the dream of my grandparents was coming true. I was wary, however, of the excesses of the nationalist fervor in Armenia, and the dangers that I had identified from a distance before my visit looked even more troublesome up close. My harshest criticism was reserved for the Armenian church. Though the increasing support of public opinion on the national question gave reason for cautious optimism, the unmistakable mark of expediency in the church's shift from partner of the central Soviet authorities and of the old Communist regime in Armenia to sacralizer of the new nationalism was worrisome indeed. It seemed clear that in return for special privileges the Armenian church was going to follow old habits and offer itself up to the new political regime as its loyal handmaid. While the church's conspicuous neglect of its spiritually starved people was distressing enough, more troubling still was the prospect of a compromised Armenian church that in the future would be unwilling or unable to call back the nation from the extremes of Armenian particularism and nationalism.

How I related to Armenian politics and how my views were perceived by those with whom I spoke was no less unsettling. In the American context, I thought of myself as a Burkean conservative. In Armenia, I was derided, even by people deeply committed to democracy, as a typically deracinated American bred on a bloodless liberalism. "What gives you Americans the right to use this word 'nationalist' against us?" exclaimed Levon Melikyan, a teacher of architecture and a self-described Christian Democrat. "Do you think love of country is bad or that we should not have the freedom that you as an American already enjoy?"

One evening, Onnig Vatyan, a former Armenian athletic star and now a school principal, drove me to the home of his sister and nephew, with whom I was staying. En route Onnig was stopped at a checkpoint. It was not necessary to understand the words that were exchanged. Onnig was trying to explain why he was out past curfew. The Russian soldiers were deliberately harassing and humiliating him in front of an American. When we were released, Onnig turned to me. In the dim light of the street lamps I saw on his face a grimace of intense, inner rage straining for utterance. "Vigen," he blurted out, "my dear friend, is this any way for human beings to live? We are like animals in a cage at the will of the zookeeper." I dug into my limited Armenian vocabulary and responded in the only way I knew how. "Onnig," I said, "every man has need of freedom, here also in Armenia." Onnig nodded, "Yes, Vigen, just so!"

The next morning Onnig drove me to his school. First, he proudly showed me the small museum of ancient artifacts that had been assembled through the generous donation of an Armenian-American philanthropist. These were the tools with which Onnig would transmit to his young charges the Armenian history, culture, and identity that had been suppressed for so long. Then he led me out onto the playground. He pointed to a trench that had been dug alongside the school building. This would be a firing range to train the youth how to defend the Armenian land from Russians, Azerbaijanis, Turks, or any other enemies that would deny them their heritage and identity.

Armenia is a microcosm of the nationalist struggles and turmoils that affect so much of the old Soviet empire and mock talk of a new world order. None of this comes as much of a surprise to those, like myself, who are connected by lineage, church, language, history, memory, and sentiment to peoples who were repressed under communism. For others in the academy, however, and for many so-called policymakers, it has been a shock. They cannot understand why these people will not be reasonable and tolerant and show respect for democracy above everything else. Even observers with a strong commitment to human rights, who are initially sympathetic, grow uneasy when they see that these movements for self-determination and nationhood are inextricably entangled with uncompromising attachment to the land, pride of nationality, and an apparently inexhaustible animosity towards historic enemies.

Of course, there have been notable exceptions to these reactions and responses. In an essay titled "Identity, Sovereignty, and Self-Determinism,"[1] Jean Bethke Elshtain cites Sir Isaiah Berlin, who in an article published thirty years ago—long before almost anyone anticipated the extraordinary events of the past decade—gave this kind of nationalism a name. He called it "bent twig" nationalism. The metaphor was intended to draw attention to a type of nationalism that is a reaction of repressed peoples to national humiliation and subjugation. Berlin argued that this kind of nationalism has its own value (independent of democratic principles) with the potential of being an important healing agent for old wounds.

Berlin's liberal credentials are hardly subject to question, so his analysis has had the effect of engendering among some of his students and admirers a tolerance of nationalism and even attempts to show that nationalism need not be antithetical to liberalism and democracy. Yael Tamir's book *Liberal Nationalism* is a case in point.[2] Tamir takes a fresh look at the historical link in the origin and development of nationalism and liberalism. She embraces Berlin's description of the psychological and historical reasons for the development of bent twig forms of nationalism, but Tamir reaches beyond a descriptive account to develop a normative theory of what she calls liberal nationalism. This theory establishes principles of autonomy, citizenship, cultural pluralism, and guarantees of the rights of minorities as criteria for judging whether a particular nationalism approximates the ideal.

Tamir justifies her normative theory with a typically liberal assessment that we live in a world in which few nations are still ethnically homogenous, and that therefore notions of peoplehood based in language, common religion, and ethnic stock are more often the products of imagination than the observation of empirical reality. She proposes liberal nationalism as a kind of halfway house between the old nation-statehood that is closely associated with political sovereignty and forms of nationhood and cultural sovereignty that are democratic and cosmopolitan. Tamir's analysis is studious, subtle, and admirably nuanced. Undoubtedly, however, my Armenian friend Levon Melikyan would see it as just a reformulated version of the same old imperious and imperialistic attitude of Western liberals who want to tell others how to behave.

In her essay, Elshtain also proposes a "middle way" between a potentially reactionary and triumphalistic cultural nationalism, on the one hand, and a bloodless liberal rationalism on the other. She is appreciative of the diversity of human culture grounded not just in reason but also in history, and she presents us with a historicist and pluralistic theory of nationhood and politics that still manages to make a strong case for upholding universal human rights. Elshtain describes this middle way as an "alternative to warring racial and ethnic groupings or the homogenized stability of efficiently managed imperialism."[3]

Elshtain's historical empiricism makes for a richer and more realistic discussion of nationalism than Tamir's, and for this reason my criticism of her position does not imply radical disagreement. I do wish to advance the view, however, that proposals for a middle way, such as those provided by Elshtain and Tamir, are not of much help at this stage. Presently, we are faced with situations that reflect unmanageable mixes of cultural nationalism, liberal democracy, populism, authoritarianism, and totalitarianism. Many of these situations are not yet amenable to a "middle way." Almost anything is possible, as long pent-up forces now contend with each other in ways that defy what we in Western liberal democracies take to be normal political processes. Our insistence on balance and compromise often blinds us to our propensity to read our own history into the struggles we observe. Too much Western analysis draws on distinctions between good guys and bad guys that are nothing more than positive and negative projections of our history and experience of liberalism and the demons that have tempted or threatened it. The national and political struggles in Russia, Ukraine, and Armenia involve very different historical choices and outcomes.

More important, however, are the assumptions that liberals bring to bear on their analysis of nationalism. I thus want to consider bent twig nationalism by initially bracketing out the liberal democratic prejudices that lie behind the rhetoric and commitments of communitarians, neoliberals, and neoconservatives alike. Their sympathy for the struggling nations of the East comes with an agenda for vindicating and advancing liberal democracy, or whatever might be saved of it in so-called postmodernity.

Elshtain draws upon Michael Ignatieff's analysis in his book, *Blood and Belonging: Journeys into the New Nationalism,* and rightly takes encouragement from Ignatieff's confession that liberals such as himself need to augment their analyses of nationalism with greater historical empiricism. One would like to think also that Ignatieff's change is a harbinger of greater openness among Western liberals to voices and events in the East that challenge their quick condemnations of nationalism and their easy assumptions about democracy as a political good. A contemporary case in point is their misinterpretation of Aleksandr Solzhenitsyn.

Solzhenitsyn was lionized by liberals in the 1960s and early 1970s. But when he came to the West as an exile from his own land and without "proper manner" proceeded to ruthlessly unmask the spiritual and ethical bankruptcy and historical illiteracy of idealistic liberal moralism, the good feelings came to an end. In his famous (or infamous) Harvard commencement address of 1978, Solzhenitsyn made it unmistakably clear that he was not a man of strict liberal civic faith, and for this the press and the academy began to depict the greatest living twentieth-century heir of the Russian polyphonic novel—Solzhenitsyn stands squarely in the tradition of Dostoevsky—as an antipluralist, antidemocratic, anti-Semitic advocate of authoritarianism.

To this day, Solzhenitsyn continues to insist on the need for inductive study of history, religious tradition, and culture rather than the accepted liberal model of deductive political reasoning. His gravest and most unforgivable sin, however, is that his God is God and not Demos. Fortunately for many in the West, Andrei Sakharov was around to fill the void left by the anathematization of Solzhenitsyn. This is not the appropriate occasion for probing what made Sakharov a more attractive and acceptable figure than Solzhenitsyn, but Elshtain has supplied a suitable analog in Václav Havel, whom she describes as an enlightened nationalist or civic patriot committed to democratic liberalism and hence worthy of our admiration. Most Western liberals who are suspicious of—or even negatively disposed toward—Solzhenitsyn would agree with her judgment concerning Havel. She accurately describes Havel's civic philosophy as dialogical, in contrast to the monological character of modern totalitarianism. Unlike many in the West, Elshtain, much to her credit, also recognizes Havel's deep and fundamental concern with religion and morality as first-order realities of human existence. He describes himself as an opponent of what he calls "the arrogant anthropocentrism of modern man."

Havel deserves this praise, and yet even he is misunderstood by secular liberals. In his case, however, these misinterpretations both reflect and reinforce a favorable bias that holds him up approvingly as a good liberal and civic patriot. Havel's beliefs are more complicated than that. The naïve accounts that portray him as a champion of Western-style democratic liberalism are the flip side of the coin that depicts Solzhenitsyn as an extreme nationalist with authoritarian tendencies. In point of fact, even though Havel's Czech nation is historically tied more closely than is Russia to the Western tradition of democratic liberalism, his worldview shares with Solzhenitsyn's many fundamental principles. For Havel's background as a dissident and opponent of Marxist-Leninism and communism make for a more complex story than the one that has been told about him by his liberal admirers in the West.

What do Solzhenitsyn and Havel believe and say in common? To begin with, both criticize modernity and the spiritual bankruptcy of advanced liberalism.[4] Both Solzhenitsyn and Havel trace the crack-up of modernity and the crisis of politics back to the crisis of faith and meaning created by the modern Promethean experiment with atheism. As early as the 1960s and 1970s, Havel recognized that the new nationalism pushing up through the cracks and rubble of a collapsing order was the valid expression of people who wanted to dig their way out. Like Solzhenitsyn, he set this impulse in the context of a much larger phenomenon affecting both East and West, the slow death of modernity. But whereas in the East we find the rubble of Marxist-Leninism, in the West it is secular liberalism, born of the Enlightenment, that is in decay.

Like Solzhenitsyn, Havel also insists that in order to recover their identity and to determine their own political systems, the peoples of the former Communist lands must return to their Christian roots, with its anthropology of the human person created in the image of God. Without this anchor the so-called democratic virtues of tolerance, compromise, and justice are like debris tossed about on a stormy sea. One can assert the value of these virtues repeatedly, but this will not make them any more capable of resisting the ethnic pride and extreme nationalism that threaten violence against neighbor and historic enemy. In 1978, Havel wrote: "To cling to the notion of traditional parliamentary democracy as one's political ideal and to succumb to the illusion that only this 'tried and true' form is capable of guaranteeing human beings enduring dignity and an independent role in society would, in my opinion, be at the very least shortsighted."[5]

That Havel has proven a friend of parliamentary democracy in no way negates his openness to new and other forms of political life and governance. This openness is based on his strong sense of history and, like Solzhenitsyn, on his ready ascription of first priority to the deeper relationship of faith and politics. Both men know the histories of their peoples. Both also recognize that even if democratic forms are preferable, the success of home-grown democratic institutions is not guaranteed by building them out of just any old democratic debris that comes floating in from America or Western Europe or anywhere else. Democracy, no less than nationalism, has its corruptions, and these occur when the inherent dignity of human beings is loaded on a ship without ballast or anchor.

Perhaps we ought to permit ourselves to hope that the solutions reached in formerly Communist countries will derive not from old expected political formulas but, rather, from larger visions of the human good that unapologetically embrace the conviction that God, not man, is the source and fountain of freedom, justice, peace, prosperity, and love, and that God, not man, is also the judge of all that we do.

I would thus end not with prognostication but with the words of an Armenian patriot and nationalist. In October 1989, soon after his release from a Soviet prison for his political activities as a member of the liberationist Karabagh Committee, Rafael Ishkhanian issued his now famous article, "The Law of Excluding the Third Force." In it, he wrote:

I think man's purpose in life is to achieve perfection. To go from bad to good, to change toward the perfect. I also think the same should be true for a nation ... to realize the mistakes of our past, to make fewer mistakes in the future....

Our path to becoming a sovereign and independent nation will become barren if we forget our Christian faith.... If we try to do everything without relying on our maker, we will fail.... We need a return to Christianity like the air we breathe. ...

I am convinced that we can survive ... if we move not with emotions and a sense of vengeance but with reason.... In this case God will help us. And if we survive, become strong, and do good deeds, our lands will be reunited to us too.

But ... if we become prisoners of our emotions, of the call of revenge, this piece of land too will be taken and we will be a lost nation.[6]

16

Human Rights and Modern Western Faith

The philosopher Richard Rorty dismisses biblical faith as myth and illusion. He has also made a career out of punching holes in Enlightenment theories that were leaky from the start. For these and other sleights of hand he has become one of the most talked about philosophers of our generation. As is evident, I am no admirer of Professor Rorty, but when he aims his criticisms at human rights doctrines and ahistorical theories of human nature, I admit that I perk up. I suppose that I too am inclined to swing an axe at some of the larger trees in the Enlightenment forest.

In other philosophical and theological quarters, too, judgments similar to Rorty's have been issued about the Enlightenment legacy and human rights, most notably by Alasdair MacIntyre and Stanley Hauerwas. MacIntyre argues that "the possession of rights [presupposes] the existence of a socially established set of rules" and that therefore "the existence of particular types of social institutions or practices is a necessary condition for ... a claim to a possession of a right ... [to be] an intelligible type of human performance."[1] I take this to mean that the only real rights are norms of human conduct that are articulated in the customs and laws of particular historical communities, a position with which I heartily agree.

I part company with all three writers, however, when they reject the notion of a normative human nature or deny that we can know about such a nature. I want to distance myself from philosophical and theological positivism regarding our *humanum*. Rorty, in particular, has gone into the ghostbusting business full force. This is a man who protests too much that he is a reasonable fellow, even while he is clearly spooked by metaphysical and epistemological specters that I am not at all sure lurk even in the dark quarters of his region of the Enlightenment wood. I am left in complete wonderment at his utter confidence that "most people—especially people relatively untouched by the European Enlightenment—simply do not think of themselves as, first and foremost, a human being." For if, as Rorty claims, these people consider themselves "as a certain *good* sort of human being—a sort defined by explicit opposition to a particularly bad sort" (Rorty 1993, 126), that very judgment surely must imply an intuition, if not a concept, of a common human nature that belongs to good as well as bad sorts of walking and talking bipeds.

Are we really supposed to take this kind of talk seriously? I do not think Rorty has got his history right or his facts straight when he makes generalizations like these—and he assaults us with them constantly. Most Orthodox Christians do not live in the West and would fit Rorty's category of persons relatively unaffected by the Enlightenment, yet they possess a strong concept of a common humanity, and we know where they got that idea. The same might be said of Muslims. The Enlightenment did not invent the concept of a universal human nature or the notion of a universal moral law, nor did Immanuel Kant or St. Thomas Aquinas or St. Augustine. What the Enlightenment did was to conjure up certain ghostly and disembodied notions of human nature and an accompanying doctrine of the "rights of man" that has become a principal source of much contemporary human rights thinking. Rorty, MacIntyre, and Hauerwas, each in his own manner, have shown us how this came about. But they risk overreaching. In their rejection of human rights, they all but dismiss the notion of a human nature and its norms. None criticizes the concept of human rights in the manner in which an Orthodox theologian is bound to do. Human rights thinking is alien to Orthodoxy; however, the notion that a normative human nature is concretely manifested in every human individual who comes into existence is central to Orthodox anthropology and theology.

Having set down these preliminary remarks, permit me to sketch out what amounts to only the most *preliminary* of clarifications. My contention is that Orthodox Christology and the vision of redemption in Orthodox theology identify what is normatively human and necessary for the freedom and flourishing of human beings in a way that is very different from that of modern human rights theory. Orthodox Christology and anthropology do not support theories of autonomous and secular human rights such as those that have emerged even within Western Christian thought.

On Christology and human rights

First, regarding Christology, I am persuaded that a strongly dyophysitic accent in mainstream Protestant and Roman Catholic Christology has contributed to what are now deeply embedded notions of human autonomy and rights in Western thought. These notions contradict Orthodoxy's insistence on the theonomous nature of humanity revealed by the divine Word's incarnate existence. From an Orthodox point of view, what is normatively human must be defined in strict accord with the creature's relationship to the divine acts of Creation and Incarnation. The humanity that the Creator Word assumed is now and forever more united with his divinity: Jesus Christ was resurrected in his body and has taken that body to his Father. This answers any doubt as to whether the good and *telos* of the human being, who is created in the image and likeness of God, may be considered apart from participation in and communion with the Divine Life itself (2 Peter 1:4). No temporal human good exists apart from a movement either toward or away from holiness and the company of the saints.

I am personally persuaded that the deepest inspiration of the doctrine of human rights has roots in Christian convictions. God is person, and so are human beings, who are created in God's image and likeness. Every human *hypostasis* has needs and makes legitimate claims to certain advantages necessary for human flourishing. *Hypostasis* is, of course, the Greek word that was adopted by the theologians of the Council of Nicaea to designate personal existence. It permitted the Council to draw the distinction between human, angelic, and divine being, while also attributing personhood to all three.

My own Armenian tradition, with its Cyrillian monophysitism—represented in the dogmatic statement "one nature, and that incarnate, of the divine Word"—has understood, from the outset of the great Christological debates of the fifth and sixth centuries, the hazards of speaking of natures or essences in the abstract, whether pertaining to the divinity or the humanity of Jesus. The Council of Nicaea had employed the term *ousia* to connote concrete existence. God is one *ousia*, one being and nature. The Son is of the same being and nature of the Father. This is how the council interpreted Jesus' words in John's Gospel: "Whosoever has seen me has seen the Father. . . . I am in the Father and the Father is in me" (14:9–10). The theologians of Nicaea employed the term *nature* in a sense analogous to what modern physics means by a *solid*. A solid, like a diamond or an ice cube, is a discrete substance that cannot be mixed into another solid in the way that one liquid or gas might be mixed with or emulsified in another.

When, at the Council of Chalcedon in 451, discussion shifted to a sharp distinction between *ousia* and *hypostasis* that entailed a language of two natures in reference to Christ, Armenians balked. This was reminiscent of Nestorianism, especially as the language of two natures appeared in Pope Leo's Tome. How could it be said, as Leo did, that "the Word performs what pertains to the Word, the flesh what pertains to the flesh" without dividing Christ in two? How could Christ be two "solids," two natures, Armenians asked, except he be two and not one? For Cyril of Alexandria, it was possible to say in the abstract that there is a *oneness* of two natures in Christ, but Leo's language suggested the impossible: a *unification* of two abstract natures in the concrete. Ultimately, my church rejected this two natures doctrine because it wanted to honor and safeguard the ancient teaching of "One Lord, one faith, one baptism" (Eph. 4:5).

What, one might ask, does this curious piece of the history of Christian doctrine have to do with how one stands on human rights? My answer is that from the standpoint of Armenian Christianity, the legacy of Western dyophysitism extends into the Enlightenment in two essentially Christian heresies: deism and the rights of man. In deism, God is removed from his creation and the Incarnation is denied, implicitly if not explicitly. In the concept of the rights of man, humanity gains an autonomy that a consistently incarnational faith will not permit. From the religious point of view, human freedom is not autonomy, that is, pure self-determination; rather, it is *autexousion,* a graced capacity to achieve full ethical personhood and mystical participation in the life of God. There is always a synergy of nature and grace.

Deism and the rights of man are late secularistic developments of a nature-grace dichotomy that crops up in the West in the medieval period and has continued into our own time. The Gelasian doctrine of the two swords, the eucharistic theology of transubstantiation, Kant's epistemology and his categorical imperative, the God of the gaps, the disembodied moral absolutes of the God of the idealists, the quest for the historical Jesus, and Rudolf Bultmann's demythologized kerygma are all expressions of this dichotomization of nature and grace.

Thus, while I respect the fact that contemporary human rights theory is not uniform—that it ranges from highly secularized interpretations to Roman Catholic Thomist renderings—from the perspective of Orthodoxy, and especially from an Armenian standpoint, the doctrine in all its varieties expresses a flawed understanding of the relation of nature and grace and of God and persons in Jesus Christ.

In his *Ethics,* Dietrich Bonhoeffer states:

> The Church's word to the world can be no other than God's word to the world. This word is Jesus Christ and salvation in His name. It is in Jesus Christ that God's relation to the world is defined.... In other words, the proper relation of the Church to the world cannot be deduced from natural law or rational law or from universal human rights, but *only* from the gospel of Jesus Christ.[2]

I agree. But permit me to reformulate this Reformed language into Orthodox speech. Human beings are not autonomous but theonomous: this is testified to in the God-man, Jesus Christ, who is no less God than human and in whom all human reality finds its being, its norm, and its fulfillment.

On redemption and human rights

The Orthodox understanding of redemption contrasts sharply with the dominant juridical and legalistic understandings of redemption predominant in the Roman Catholic and Protestant traditions. I am referring especially to the notion of atonement as satisfaction given to God, which often carries a strong penal meaning. I can only begin to suggest the profound difference it makes for Christian social ethics whether one holds primarily to the physicalist Orthodox vision of redemption as cure of sin and death that takes place *within* the creature or whether one adopts Western understandings of redemption as earned or imputed righteousness in which an inward change is not as significant as the claim to a change of the creature's *position* in relation to God.

I am painting with a broad brush. I am aware that much detail work would be expected of a fuller treatment. Yet it does seem to me logical and perhaps inevitable that a civilization in which the latter views of redemption prevailed would turn to a "solution" to human suffering in which justice (*jus*) and law supplant holiness and righteousness as the supreme objects of Christian striving. Nevertheless, as the Russian religious philosopher Nicholas Berdyaev rightly observed, "Redemption is . . . not [firstly] the reconciliation between God and man." It is, rather, the destruction "of the roots of sin and evil" in the heart of being.[3] Redemption is not first about human or divine justice but about cure of sin and victory over death; against these, death and sin combined, an ethics of law alone is quite impotent.

Accordingly, in Orthodox theology and ethics, the social imperative that stems from redemption in Jesus Christ is not initially a call to political or legal action, but the much more radical call to repentance and self-limitation. Repentance is the principal evidence of a deep inner conversion of heart, of *metanoia*. Humility (in Hebrew *'ânâh* and in Greek *tapeinos*), not justice (or *jus*), is the highest virtue of Orthodox ethics. Humility born out of repentance combats self-love and is the balm that heals wounded pride. The counterpart of humility in political ethics is the magnanimity that curbs vengeance and the ever-present will to power.

Fr. Alexander Men was a Russian Orthodox priest martyred for his faith in 1990. In his sermons and writings, Men applied this Orthodox understanding of redemption as conversion and cure to his profound social concerns. He made it the cornerstone of his social gospel. Consider the following excerpt from an interview that Fr. Men gave shortly before he was brutally murdered with an axe. He said:

> I believe that just as in previous ages, people emerged to lead
> the world out of its spiritual dead end, so in our times too the
> right people will be found. And as regards repentance, the
> good news of Christ was preceded by a call to repentance;

this is what John the Baptist called people to. And the very first word of Jesus' teaching was "Repent." And remember that in Hebrew this word means "turn around," "turn away from the wrong road." While in the Greek text of the Gospels, it is rendered by an even more resonant word, *metanoite*, in other words *rethink* your life. This is the beginning of healing. Repentance is not a sterile "grubbing around in one's soul," not some masochistic self-humiliation, but a re-evaluation leading to action, the action John the Baptist called "the fruits of repentance."

That's why there is so much hope in the numerous attempts now being made to rethink our recent history, to "change our minds." The abscess must be lanced, otherwise there will be no cure.[4]

Alexander Solzhenitsyn also speaks out of this Orthodox Christian vision of redemption:

"Human rights" are a fine thing, but [the difficult question is] how can we ourselves make sure that our rights do not expand at the expense of the rights of others. A society with unlimited rights is incapable of standing to adversity. If we do not wish to be ruled by a coercive authority, then each of us must rein himself in. . . . A stable society [and world] is achieved not by balancing opposing forces but by conscious self-limitation: by the principle that we are always duty-bound to defer to the sense of moral justice.

Solzhenitsyn makes mention of human rights rarely, and when he does, he is usually addressing Western ears or Western concerns; more often than not, what he means by "human rights" are civil rights and liberties protected in law. The questions he raises, however, about the use of the rhetoric of human rights issue a challenge. If the sin and woundedness that are in each one of us are not first cured, if healing has not begun, then human rights rhetoric will do little good. If repentance and forgiveness do not fill the brittle shell of this ethical and legal formalism, how can sinful human beings resist turning their claims to human rights into swords of vengeance or into injurious pretexts for self-aggrandizement? What is to prevent even the championing of the rights of the oppressed from becoming an exercise in self-righteous self-magnification?

These are some of the weaknesses and hazards that a full-blown Orthodox critique of human rights doctrine would identify. It would address and seek to remedy these shortcomings, not with a refurbished doctrine of human rights, but rather with a biblical anthropology that rests human freedom and dignity squarely in God's own Being and the Second Person of the Trinity. In Revelation we read that Jesus Christ is "the Lamb slain from the foundation of the world" (13:8). This presents us with the profound mystery that our humanity belongs to the Son from eternity. The *imago Dei* includes his eternal humanity. By his Incarnation the Son has revealed to us the full measure of our humanity (Ephesians 4:13).

Some argue that human rights stand on their own and do not "need" God or religion. This compounds the error of their doctrine. Our *humanum* is grounded in God's being and activity. Human existence is theonomous by origin and nature. A humanity that claims autonomy or professes atheism is fallen, sinful, and incomplete. To believe in the Incarnation is to believe that not only God exists as God, but also that God is human. Likewise, by his life, death, resurrection, and ascension, Jesus Christ has revealed the true purpose and goal of our freedom and dignity. The Incarnate Word of God leads humanity to complete participation in the divine life (2 Peter 1:3–4) and unhindered communion with the three Divine Persons, One God.

Here, briefly, I have endeavored to set down the important reasons why Eastern Orthodoxy does not invest much of its theological or moral capital in the modern doctrine of human rights. I have ventured this argument knowing full well that it challenges the belief held by many that a commitment to human rights necessarily follows from Christian faith. To this I am bound to respond: "Sisters and brothers, it simply is not so."

17

Human Rights and
Christian Ethics

I have no party in this business, my dear Miss Palmer, but among a
set of people, who have none of your Lillies and Roses in their faces;
but who are the images of the great Pattern as well as you and I. I
know what I am doing; whether the white people like it or not.[1]

— Edmund Burke

D avid Little and I have been friends for nearly twenty years,
and for just about that long we have been carrying on an
argument about human rights—he the advocate, and I the
skeptic. David is a genuine liberal, an endangered species
today. In fact, I am not sure which is the more endangered,
his kind of Calvinistic and Kantian liberalism, or my kind of Cappadocian
and Burkean conservatism.

But we are living in strange times, or at least I feel as if I am living in
a strange time, because I find that at the beginning of the third millen-
nium what I share in common with old-fashioned religious liberals like
David Little matters a lot. Like some of them, I am extremely discom-
forted by what the new breed of postmodernists are saying. I find myself
standing alongside them in opposition to the outrageous notion held by
some writers in Christian ethics that there is no such thing as human na-

ture or a moral law. One expects to hear negations of this sort from the likes of Richard Rorty, but not from Alasdair MacIntyre or Stanley Hauerwas.

And so, while I do not often look into Locke's *Second Treatise* or Kant's *Groundwork of the Metaphysics of Morals,* I am bound to respond in the spirit of Edmund Burke to our present crop of secularistic and religious communitarians. At the trial of Warren Hastings, the corrupt British Governor-General of Bengal, Burke condemned Britain's ruthless exploitation of the people of India. Burke vehemently protested what he called the new "geographical morality" that Hastings and his defenders had proposed in order to justify the rape of an ancient and noble civilization. They claimed that "the duties of men, in public and in private situations, are not to be governed by their relation to the great Governor of the Universe, or by their relation to mankind, but by climate, degrees of longitude, parallels, not of life, but of latitudes: as if, when you have crossed the equinoctial, all the virtues die." Burke responded with the argument "that the laws of morality are the same everywhere, and that there is no action which would pass for extortion, of peculation, of bribery, of oppression in England that is not the . . . [same] in Europe, Asia, Africa, and all the world over. This I contend for," he insisted, "not in the technical form of it, but for it in the substance."[2]

I am opposed to ethical relativism under whatever label it comes. I affirm the epistemological realism and universalistic anthropology of historic Christianity over and against postliberal and postmodernist negations. I recently came upon this passage in a collection of the nineteenth-century Anglican theologian F. D. Maurice's writings. It eloquently affirms our common humanity in classical Christian terms:

> [God] is emphatically *not* a capricious Being who interferes on behalf of a few favourites, but one who had made himself known to men through a Son—that Son entering into the nature of men, dying the death of men, rising for men, exalting

His manhood at the right hand of God, being the Head and Judge of men. Here is the common Humanity of men; here is that Humanity exhibited not in some partial examples, but in a Central Object to whom all may turn, in whom all may see their own perfection.[3]

This is the Christian inheritance to which Edmund Burke made reference in the magnificent passage with which I have prefaced this chapter.

That some contemporary Christian ethicists have embraced the basic philosophical premises of postmodernism may be leading to something far more troublesome than even the sort of theological positivism of which Karl Barth sometimes was accused. Might it be an invitation to a new Christian nihilism? Could the new religious communitarianism and the postmodernist paean for pragmatic pluralism be a dress rehearsal for increased intercommunal conflict, where power is not ashamed to prowl naked and stalk the weak, and conflicting collective egoisms lay waste to civil societies? No one need explain the horror of such conflict to Ottoman Armenians, European Jews, the Tutsis of Rwanda, the Christians of Indonesia, the Bosnian Muslims, or the Darfuris of Sudan. Who knows, our turn may yet be coming; we too may be visited by a demonic fury that willfully wreaks its awful destruction on a culture from which belief in a common humanity and a universal moral law has been evacuated.

And yet, my disagreements with religious liberals are nearly as profound. They include a very different assessment than that given by most liberals of the crisis in Christian ethics, and also a serious skepticism about the modern human rights project to which liberals are committed. In this chapter I want to try to specify these differences. My remarks comprise four related points:

First, while I am willing to concede the assertion of religious liberals like David Little that the *concept* of human rights is gaining legitimacy in many places throughout the world, I am not inclined to put the same hope in that trend.

On August 23, 1990, the first democratically elected Armenian parliament of the post-Soviet era issued its Declaration on Armenia's Independence. Here is the relevant text:

> Expressing the united will of the Armenian people;
>
> Aware of its historic responsibility for the destiny of the Armenian people and engaged in the realization of the aspirations of all Armenians and the restoration of historical justice;
>
> Proceeding from the principles of the Universal Declaration of Human Rights and the generally recognized norms of international law;
>
> Exercising the right of nations to free self-determination...
>
> [and the text continues].[4]

Appeals like this to the Universal Declaration are not uncommon among newly emerging nations. No doubt at the time that the Declaration of Armenian Independence was issued there were also strong practical considerations about world opinion that entered into the choice of language. Power quite consciously was being addressed, the power of America and Europe that Armenians hoped might be enlisted to persuade Russia to loosen its control over their nation. However, it would be a cynical and grievous mistake to assume that this consideration of power was all that motivated Armenians to invoke the Universal Declaration. For a variety of reasons, some unique to Armenia, with its tragic modern history of genocide and diaspora, these moral and political principles may have found a more hospitable home there than in neighboring Azerbaijan. Yet serious irregularities in presidential and parliamentary elections as recently as 2003, restrictions on opposition parties, an accumulation of executive branch power bordering on authoritarianism, and a consistently poor human rights record on several fronts place this claim in doubt. Similar difficulties and reversals have arisen in other former Soviet republics, such as Belarus, the Ukraine, and Russia itself, where in the 1990s democracy and human rights principles seemed to have had promise.

David Little identifies a dilemma faced by many nations that have claimed to respect human rights. He asks, "How are nations who are in part, at least, committed to universal, nondiscriminatory standards to reconcile or harmonize those standards with countervailing indigenous standards" and, in the worst cases, legal, judicial, and political structures that routinely violate these standards? His own answer to that question is that "regardless of whatever compromises are respectively worked out," it is unlikely that over the long term these nations "will be able to escape the grip of the human rights vocabulary that, for very important historical reasons, now is embedded in their collective consciousness."[5]

I am not persuaded of Little's conclusion. As willing as I might be to concede that the concept of human rights has made significant inroads into the political consciousness of some nations, I do not think this forecasts anything strongly one way or the other for the future. I am not sure the liberal theory of human rights has much staying power outside of certain historic political societies in which a deeply embedded tradition of democratic constitutionalism and the rule of law already exists. And while in some places liberty and justice make gains, in other places the autochthonic powers of racism, sexism, and tyranny arise and stalk humanity with new ferocity, easily overwhelming paper declarations of human rights.

My second point is closely related to the first. Could it be that liberal Protestantism's spirit of benevolence and its faith in reason and democratic progress has migrated out of ecclesial quarters and found a new home in the international human rights movement? This makes for some interesting speculation. David Little's personal history is strongly suggestive of such a pattern. He hails from a long line of prominent Presbyterian church leaders. His grandparents' generation of missionaries heroically saved tens of thousands of Armenian lives during World War I when the Ottoman Turkish government prosecuted its vicious plan to exterminate the Armenians of Turkey. That missionary zeal resides still in liberals like David Little. They want to save and improve people's lives, and they pursue this aim through international human rights organizations. This is the nobility in the liberal cause, and, I would add, the Christian heart in it.

But my Armenian tragic memory is strong, and my American psyche is underdeveloped. From the perspective of Armenians, Serbs, or Greek Cypriots, none of whom lack guilt for having spilt the innocent blood of their neighbors, but all of whom endured enormous losses of human life in the twentieth century, that century did not witness an increase in morality or justice. The modern human rights project has yet to show that it makes a believable difference. Even among Armenians, the embrace of human rights sometimes seems more like the expression of a desperate hope than anything else. There is a quiet, inner Armenian voice, which on occasion rises to a shrill scream, that questions whether these rational norms can ever really shield Armenians against intractable ethnic animosities, old religious hatreds, and collective scapegoating. Almost always the Western advocates of human rights have failed to put their muscle where their mouths are; sometimes human rights moralism has undone vital balances of power. Sometimes such moralism has been rendered impotent by Western economic interests, not to say greed. Are human rights any less subject to misuse than the best teachings of the historic religions on love and respect for one's fellows? Indeed, there is an historic debate in Armenia over whether to trust in the "Third Force." The first force is the Armenians themselves, the second is their neighbors. The "Third Force" is Western-style liberalism and its patrons. That debate is not closed.

So while my sentiments are with the basic affirmations about morality and the human good that move religious and secular liberals to promote the modern human rights project, as an Orthodox Christian I am bound to raise some serious questions about that project's philosophical foundations as well as the much repeated assertion that it represents the best hope for peace and justice in the contemporary world. I am not speaking merely in practical terms or about balances of power. No, there is a real question about the human rights movement: Is it, in itself, fundamentally ill conceived?

This brings me to my third and most radical point. I am persuaded that the human rights project has not only become an essentially secularist scheme, but that its impetus is atheistic. This does not mean religious people cannot find value in human rights. I am not ignoring nor am I discounting the fact that many Christians have embraced the language of human rights and that this has given force to movements of liberation in Eastern Europe, Africa, Latin America, the Philippines, and elsewhere. However, such commitments by Christians to the human rights agenda do not in themselves dispel or disprove my thesis about its inherently secularist nature.

What seems to be true is that the Christian faith made possible the modern conception of human rights. Historic Christianity lent to a culture its profound convictions about human dignity and individual and social freedom. Such convictions were and are rooted in the Incarnation and a belief in a triune God. The theology of the cross and belief in the resurrection strengthened an awareness of human suffering and provided the motivation to remedy it. Nevertheless, if one joins the modern human rights project, powerful forces would have one eschew these religious convictions, or at least subordinate them in deference to so-called objective norms of reason and positive law. We are told, in effect, that practical reason can do without the Decalogue but must embrace the formulations of the Universal Declaration of Human Rights. It is not that the human rights project cannot agree with much that is in the Decalogue. It is that this project ultimately refuses to honor God, certainly in any public way. This is a practical atheism at best. Indeed, among many secular people who nevertheless have faith in modern human rights, denial of the God of the Decalogue is part of that faith. The denial of God permits the affirmation of humanity. Religious persons who think that this still leaves enough room for common ground may be fooling themselves, perhaps not in the practical present, but almost certainly in the faithless future.

Lest there be misunderstanding, I am not preparing to argue that biblical faith is the only possible foundation of universal human rights and, therefore, Christians ought to reestablish their ascendancy in this regard. My point is far more modest. Let me state it in the negative, so as to underscore the priority of faith. If human beings do not worship and pray and repent, then human rights are already deeply in trouble. Please understand what I mean by repentance. Repentance is not merely a sense of guilt or a guilt complex about not having lived up to the potential of one's humanity or having served humanity well enough. That is the stuff of an insipid moralism. Even the individual sense of sinfulness is not yet repentance. Repentance is asking God's forgiveness for having denied one's creaturely limits and having misused one's freedom in contravention of God's law, with harm done to oneself and injustice done to others. True repentance is the recognition of one's sins, understood as such in light of God's righteousness; and it is the pursuit of new goals, framed in the hope of God's mercy.

In his remarkable essay "Repentance and Self-Limitation," Aleksandr Solzhenitsyn remarks: "The gift of repentance, which perhaps more than anything else distinguishes man from the animal world, is particularly difficult for modern man to recover. We have, every last one of us, grown ashamed of this feeling; and its effect on *social* life everywhere on earth is less and less easy to discern."[6] Yet the hope for a better future, Solzhenitsyn believes, depends entirely upon the cultivation of a discipline of personal repentance and its transference from individual to social life. "We have so bedeviled the world, brought it so close to self-destruction," he concludes, "that repentance is now a matter of life and death—not for the sake of life beyond the grave (which is thought merely comical these days), but for the sake of our life here and now."[7]

I fear that autonomous reason is what the modern human rights project is really about, not biblical faith, and certainly not the existence of God or a recognition of our sinfulness before the Creator and our need to repent. In this respect, I wonder if the effort to survey religious belief and demonstrate that religion can play a positive role in the promotion of human rights may already be a rearguard action against much more powerful antireligious forces. For I also suspect that the reason why offenses against so-called religious human rights are among the most ignored by governments is that an already deeply institutionalized atheism is at the source.

Autonomous reason is a creature of what Orthodox theology calls the fallen gnomic will and is thoroughly subject to corruption, capable of lending infinite justifications to the *libido dominandi*. Paradoxically, the twin horn of a reason that affirms its own autonomy is an irrationalism that defies subservience to reason's *nomos*. This is our present situation. We are caught between the twin horns of a beast that is the atheism of our own creation, a dark shadow of our own enormous pride and arrogance. Václav Havel minces no words about this:

> We are going through a great departure from God which has no parallel in history. As far as I know, we are living in the middle of the first atheistic civilization. . . . I feel that this arrogant anthropocentrism of modern man who is convinced he can know everything and bring everything under his control, is somewhere in the background of the present crisis. . . .
>
> Man must in some way come to his senses. . . . He must discover again, within himself, a deeper sense of responsibility toward the world, which means responsibility toward something higher than himself. . . . The power to awaken this new responsibility is beyond [the] reach [of the physical and human sciences]. . . . It may seem like a paradox, but . . . only through directing ourselves toward the moral and the spiritual, based on respect for some "extramundane" authority—for the order of nature or the universe, for a moral order and its suprapersonal origin, for the absolute—can we arrive at a state in which life on this earth is no longer threatened by some form of "megasuicide."[8]

My fourth and last point can be made briefly. It is about the sense that one can make of the concept of human rights from the standpoint of my own Orthodox Christianity. I regard the rights named in the Universal Declaration and other modern documents as heuristic instruments that help us to identify (1) the real needs and advantages necessary for human flourishing, including the body and the spirit, and (2) the duties and responsibilities that human beings owe one another in order that these needs and advantages might be secured. These needs and advantages have been identified through the long course of the collective experience of humanity. What we call "human rights" reflect the laws and customs of nations, by which the human race has more and less successfully articulated the normativity of what it means to be human. Human nature and its relationship to the highest value of human and divine personhood were fully revealed in Jesus Christ, but others outside of that faith are not without some knowledge of the same.

The justice that would be measured by so-called universal human rights is historically embodied justice and never more than a rough approximation of the righteousness and love of the kingdom of God. But this justice is, nevertheless, real because God is real and God keeps his promises, and because freedom and justice belong to God's eternal covenant with us.

"Freedom is *self-restriction!* Restriction of the self for the sake of others."[9] "[And] justice exists even if there are only a few individuals who recognize it as such. [Because] there is nothing relative about justice, as there is nothing relative about conscience. Indeed justice is conscience, not a personal conscience but the conscience of the whole of humanity."[10] These are Solzhenitsyn's words. They eloquently express the ancient wisdom of the Orthodox Church on freedom and justice. This wisdom forms the basis of the social gospel of Orthodox Christianity. If this gospel is proclaimed by the prophet, preached by the church, and developed in every sector of life within the Orthodox lands that have been liberated from Soviet tyranny, it will do far more to preserve human dignity than all the lists of human rights enshrined in our modern documents. This is so because the kingdom of God is more real than any theory of justice formulated by human beings at any given moment in history, including the modern concept of human rights. In Christ Jesus, the kingdom walked among us in the Person of the eternal Word. Every time the church baptizes a human being, a new ecclesial person is born in Christ's likeness with the eternal marks of the church—wholeness, holiness, catholicity, and apostolicity—sealed in that person by the Spirit, inaugurating the kingdom anew. And whenever Christians gather around the Lord's table, say His prayer, and receive the holy offerings, they participate in the freedom and love and joy of the kingdom of God.

The Victorian writer George MacDonald says in one of his sermons that "Obedience is the opener of the eyes."[11] Perhaps if we were more obedient to him whom we call Lord, our eyes might return to the kingdom of God, where they belong. And I imagine that if we did that, Christian ethics might better comprehend what is most valuable and worth defending in the modern human rights doctrine, and we might stand a better chance of protecting and improving the lives of our brothers and sisters all over this earth.

Notes

Chapter 1: G. K. Chesterton: Rallying the Really Human Things

1. Gilbert K. Chesterton, *The Thing* (New York: Sheed and Ward, 1930), 22.
2. *The Collected Works of G. K. Chesterton*, ed. Lawrence J. Clipper, vol. 35, *The Illustrated London News* 1929–1931 (San Francisco: Ignatius Press, 1991), 84.
3. Gregory Wolfe, *The New Religious Humanists* (New York: Free Press, 1997), xi.
4. Ibid., xv.
5. Chesterton, *The Thing*, 34.
6. Jacques Maritain, *Integral Humanism* (Notre Dame, IN: University of Notre Dame Press, 1973), 21.
7. Chesterton, *Orthodoxy*, 32.
8. Ibid., 22.
9. Ibid., 30.
10. Ibid., *Orthodoxy*, 36–37.

11. G. K. Chesterton, *Heretics* (New York: John Lane Company, 1905), 25.

12. Ibid., 26–27.

13. Ibid., 32.

14. Ibid., 33.

15. Joseph Wood Krutch, *The Modern Temper*, (New York: Harcourt, Brace and Company, 1929), xv–xvi.

16. Ibid., 247.

17. Ibid., 137, 142.

18. Ibid., 249.

19. Ibid.

20. Ibid., 229.

21. See, for example, *Orthodoxy*, 37.

22. Chesterton, *Heretics*, 37.

23. Ibid., 286.

24. Robert Royal, "Christian Humanism in a Postmodern Age," in *The New Religious Humanists*, 103.

25. Chesterton, *Heretics*, 304–05.

Chapter 2: Flannery O'Connor: The Art of Incarnation

1. Flannery O'Connor, *Mystery and Manners* (New York: Farrar, Straus and Giroux, 1969), 68.

2. Ibid., *Mystery and Manners*, 148.

3. Flannery O'Connor, *The Habit of Being*, ed. Sally Fitzgerald (New York: Farrar, Straus and Giroux, 1979), 300.

4. O'Connor, *Mystery and Manners*, 165.

5. Ibid., 163.

6. Flannery O'Connor, *The Complete Stories* (New York: Farrar, Straus and Giroux, 1992), 376.

7. Ibid., 373.

8. Ibid., 382.

9. Ibid., 367.

10. O'Connor, *Mystery and Manners*, 82.

11. O'Connor, *Complete Stories,* 382.

12. Ibid., 518.

13. Ibid., 513.

14. Ibid., 512–13.

15. Ibid., 513.

16. Ibid., 514.

17. Ibid.

18. Ibid., 519.

19. Ibid., 520.

20. Ibid., 522.

21. Ibid., 529–30.

22. Kathleen Feeley, *Voice of the Peacock* (New York: Fordham University Press, 1982), 150–51.

23. O'Connor, *Habit of Being,* 341.

24. O'Connor, *Mystery and Manners,* 68.

Chapter 3: Russell Kirk: Christian Humanism and Conservatism

1. Russell Kirk, *Redeeming the Time* (Wilmington, DE: ISI Books, 1996), 15.

2. Maisie Ward, *Gilbert Keith Chesterton* (London: Sheed and Ward, 1944), 245.

3. Russell Kirk, *The Sword of Imagination: Memoirs of a Half-Century of Literary Conflict* (Grand Rapids, MI: Wm. B. Eerdmans Publishing Co., 1995), 202.

4. Kirk, *Dreams of Avarice*, 338. Russell Kirk's strong appreciation for Pico is bound to be controversial. Pico is subject to various conflicting interpretations: as one of the more conservative Christian humanists, on the one hand, and as a radical Pelagian and precursor of all that goes wrong with modernity, its rationalism and naïve faith in human progress, on the other. I cannot negotiate fully this controversy here. But this much needs to be said: Pico is neither an Augustinian nor a Calvinist, but that does not make him a Pelagian, unless

one classifies Eastern Christianity as Pelagian. Neo-Platonism and Pseudo-Dionysius influence Pico. Man is microcosm and possesses a gift of freedom attributable to the *imago Dei*. This is man's dignity. Thus, Pico holds to a doctrine of human perfection much akin to the Eastern Christian doctrine of *theosis* (growth in the likeness of God into eternal life). I especially disagree with John Passmore, who, in *The Perfectibility of Man* (New York: Charles Scribner's Sons, 1970), maintains that according to Pico "man is born . . . without a nature but with the capacity to choose what nature he will adopt." And it is absurd to say, as Passmore goes on to claim, that Pico's anthropology approximates that of Sartre (see p. 104 of Passmore's book). This is wrong because, as Kirk demonstrates, Pico's anthropology is based in biblical and orthodox Christian belief in the *imago Dei*. Humanity may grow and ascend to the likeness of the humanity of God in Jesus Christ or descend into the brutish and demonic. Only in this sense is human nature "indeterminate."

5. Ibid., 336–37.

6. Ibid., 337.

7. Ibid., 338.

8. Ibid., 339.

9. Ibid.

10. Ibid., 337.

11. Kirk, *Sword of Imagination*, 231, 230.

12. William F. Buckley, *Nearer, My God: Autobiography of Faith* (New York: Doubleday, 1997), 124.

13. Portions of this section are taken nearly verbatim form my introduction to Russell Kirk, *Ancestral Shadows: An Anthology of Ghostly Tales* (Grand Rapids, MI: Wm. B. Eerdmans Publishing Co., 2004).

14. Kirk, *Ancestral Shadows*, 402.

15. Ibid., 5.

16. Ibid.

17. Ibid., 16.

18. Ibid., 16–17.

19. Ibid., 394.

20. Ibid., 276, 277–78.

21. Ibid., 278.
22. Kirk, *Redeeming the Time*, 309.
23. Kirk, *Dreams of Avarice*, 177.
24. Russell Kirk, *Rights and Duties: Reflections on Our Conservative Constitution* (Dallas: Spence Publishing, 1997), 187.
25. Kirk, *Dreams of Avarice*, 339.
26. Russell Kirk, *Decadence and Renewal in the Higher Education: An Episodic History of the American University and College since 1953* (South Bend, IN: Gateway Editions, 1978), 63.
27. Russell Kirk, *A Program for Conservatives* (Chicago: Henry Regnery Co., 1954), 99.
28. Russell Kirk, *The Conservative Mind* (Chicago: Henry Regnery Co., 1953), 7–8.
29. T. S. Eliot, "Second Thoughts About Humanism," in *T. S. Eliot: Selected Essays* (London and Boston: Faber and Faber, 1963), 485.
30. Ibid.
31. Russell Kirk, Introduction to Irving Babbitt, *Literature and the American College* (Washington, DC: National Humanities Institute, 1986), 58.
32. Ibid., 10.
33. Ibid., 59.
34. Ibid., 59–60.
35. Russell Kirk, *Eliot and His Age: T. S. Eliot's Moral Imagination in the Twentieth Century* (New York: Random House, 1971), 140.

Chapter 6: The Lost Children

1. John Saward, *The Way of the Lamb: The Spirit of Childhood and the End of the Age* (San Francisco: Ignatius Press, 1999); Henry A. Giroux, *Stealing Innocence: Youth, Corporate Power, and the Politics of Culture* (New York: St. Martin's Press, 2000).

Chapter 9: Family and Virtue in a Post-Christian World: The Vision of John Chrysostom

1. John Chrysostom, *St. John Chrysostom on Marriage and Family Life*, trans. Catherine P. Roth and David Anderson (Crestwood, NY: St. Vladimir's Seminary Press, 1986), 57.

2. Ibid., 44.

3. Stanley Hauerwas and William H. Willimon, *Resident Aliens: Life in the Christian Colony* (Nashville, TN: Abingdon Press, 1990), 45–46.

4. Gerhardt B. Ladner, *The Idea of Reform* (New York: Harper and Row, 1967), 125.

5. Ibid., 126.

6. Ibid., 125–26.

7. Ibid., 127.

8. Ibid., 129.

9. Ibid.

10. I have learned much about this from Gus George Christo's dissertation, "The Church's Identity Established Through Images According to St. John Chrysostom" (Ph.D. dissertation, University of Durham, 1990). Christo's work has alerted me to a number of passages that I cite from Chrysostom below.

11. John Chrysostom, *The Homilies of St. John Chrysostom on the Acts of the Apostles*, in *A Select Library of Nicene and Post-Nicene Fathers of the Christian Church*, First Series, vol. 11 (Grand Rapids, MI: Wm. B. Eerdmans Publishing Co., 1956), 277 (homily 26).

12. Ibid., 127 (homily 26).

13. Chrysostom, *Chrysostom on Marriage*, 103–04.

14. Chrysostom, *Homilies on Acts*, 276 (homily 45).

15. John Chrysostom, "First Epistle of St. Paul the Apostle to the Corinthians," in *The Homilies of St. John Chrysostom*, Part II (Oxford and London: John Henry Parker, J. G. F. and J. Rivington, 1839), 620.

16. Christo, "Church's Identity," 386.

17. I have used Emilianos Timiadis's translation of this passage as it appears in his "Restoration and Liberation in and by the Community," *Greek Orthodox*

Theological Review, vol. 19, no. 2 (Autumn 1974), 54. See also John Chrysostom, *Homilies on the Gospel of St. Matthew,* in *A Select Library of Nicene and Post-Nicene Fathers of the Christian Church,* vol. 10 (Grand Rapids, MI: Wm. B. Eerdmans Publishing Co., 1956), 434–35 (homily 71).

18. John Chrysostom, *A Comparison Between a King and a Monk; Against the Opponents of the Monastic Life: Two Treatises,* trans. David G. Hunter (Lewiston, NY: Edwin Mellon Press, 1988), 171 (book 3).

19. Ibid., 171–72.

20. Chrysostom, *Chrysostom on Marriage,* 67.

21. Ibid., 68.

22. Ibid.

23. Ibid.

24. *The Blessing of Marriage or The Canon of the Rite of Holy Matrimony According to the Usage of the Armenian Apostolic Orthodox Church* (New York: Armenian Church Publications, 1953), 56.

25. Chrysostom, *Opponents of Monastic Life,* 172.

26. Chrysostom, *Chrysostom on Marriage,* 68.

27. Elizabeth Schüssler Fiorenza, *In Memory of Her* (New York: Crossroad Publishing Co., 1988), esp. 266–70.

28. John H. Yoder, *The Politics of Jesus* (Grand Rapids, MI: Wm. B. Eerdmans Publishing Co., 1972), esp. 174–75, 180–81, 190–92.

29. Fiorenza, *Memory,* 270.

30. Chrysostom, *Chrysostom on Marriage,* 45.

31. Ibid., 58.

32. Ibid., 46.

33. Ibid., 47.

34. Ibid., 48.

35. Ibid., 47.

36. Chrysostom, *Chrysostom on Marriage,* 69.

37. Chrysostom, *An Address on Vainglory and the Right Way for Parents to Bring Up Their Children,* appended to L. W. Laistner, *Christianity and Pagan Culture* (Ithaca, NY: Cornell University Press, 1951), 106–07.

38. Chrysostom, *Chrysostom on Marriage,* 69.

39. See, for example, James and Kathleen McGinnis, "The Social Mission of the Family," in *Faith and Families*, ed. Lindell Sawyers (Philadelphia: Geneva Press, 1986), 89–113.

40. Chrysostom, *Chrysostom on Marriage*, 71.

Chapter 15: Nationalism, A Non-Liberal Assessment

1. Elshtain's essay first appeared in Luis E. Lugo, ed., *Sovereignty at the Crossroads? Morality and International Politics in the Post-Cold War Era* (Lanham, MD: Rowman and Littlefield, 1996). This chapter also first appeared in that collection.

2. Yael Tamir, *Liberal Nationalism* (Princeton, NJ: Princeton University Press, 1993).

3. Elshtain, "Identity, Sovereignty, and Self-Determinism," 110.

4. For an informative discussion of these commonalities, see Edward E. Ericson, Jr., *Solzhenitsyn and the Modern World* (Washington, DC: Regnery Gateway, 1993), especially chap. 13.

5. Václav Havel, "The Power of the Powerless," in *Open Letters: Selected Writings 1965–1990* (New York: Vintage Books, 1992), 209.

6. Rafael Ishkhanian, "The Law of Excluding the Third Force," in *Armenia at the Crossroads: Democracy and Nationhood in the Post-Soviet Era*, ed. Gerard J. Libaridian (Watertown, MA: Blue Crane Books, 1991), 10, 36, 38.

Chapter 17: Human Rights and Modern Western Faith

1. Alasdair MacIntyre, *After Virtue*. 2nd edition (Notre Dame, IN: University of Notre Dame Press, 1984), 67.

2. Dietrich Bonhoeffer, *Ethics*. Translated by Neville Horton Smith (New York: Macmillan Company, 1965 [1949]), 357.

3. Nicholas Berdyaev, *The Destiny of Man*. Translated by Natalie Duddington (New York: Harper and Row, 1960 [1931]), 103, 104.

4. Alexander Men, *Christianity for the Twenty-first Century* (New York: Continuum, 1996), 142.

5. Aleksandr Solzhenitsyn, *Rebuilding Russia* (New York: Farrar, Straus and Giroux, 1991), 54.

Chapter 18: Human Rights and Christian Ethics

1. Edmund Burke to Mary Palmer on January 19, 1786, regarding the impeachment of Warren Hastings for crimes committed against the people of India.
2. Edmund Burke, *Speeches in the Impeachment of Warren Hastings. The Works of the Right Honorable Edmund Burke,* vol. 9 (Boston: Little, Brown, and Company 1899), 448.
3. F. D. Maurice, *Reconstructing Christian Ethics: Selected Writings,* ed. Ellen K. Wondra (Louisville, KY: Westminster John Knox, 1995), 165.
4. *Declaration of Armenia's Independence by the Armenian Parliment* in *Armenia at the Crossroads,* ed Gerard J. Libaridian (Watertown, MA: Blue Crane Books, 1991), 108.
5. David Little, "The Nature and Basis of Human Rights," in *Prospects for a Common Morality,* eds. Gene Outka and John P. Reered, Jr. (Princeton, NJ: Princeton University Press, 1993), 77.
6. Alexander Solzhenitsyn, *From Under the Rubble* (New York: Bantam Books, Inc., 1976), 106.
7. Solzhenitsyn, *From Under the Rubble,* 106.
8. Vaclav Havel, *Disturbing the Peace,* trans. Paul Wilson (New York: Alfred A. Knopf, 1990), 11–12.
9. Solzhenitsyn, *From Under the Rubble,* 136.
10. Quoted in Edward E. Ericson, Jr., *Solzhenitsyn and the World* (Washington, DC: Regnery Gateway, 1993), 28.
11. C. S. Lewis, ed. *George MacDonald: An Anthology* (New York: Simon and Schuster, 1996), 28.

Index

About the Author

Vigen Guroian is Professor of Theology at Loyola College in Maryland. He is the author of numerous articles and books, including *Ethics after Christendom: Toward an Ecclesial Christian Ethic* and *Tending the Heart of Virtue: How Classic Stories Awaken a Child's Imagination.*